Praise for *Living a Blessed Life*

"*Living a Blessed Life* is an extraordinary book that guides you through the process of attracting wealth and living an abundant life. The book is simple to read and filled with profound financial spiritual principles that anyone who reads them and puts them into use will see their lives transformed immediately."

—Louis Barajas, financial expert to the underserved and author of *Small Business, Big Life*

"Lisa Horuczi Markus offers an inspiring guide to redefining your relationship with money, recasting your definition of an abundant life, and embracing the liberation that comes from building spiritual wealth. Blessed advice indeed."

—Laura Rowley, author of *Money & Happiness: A Guide to Living the Good Life* and personal finance columnist for *Self* magazine and Yahoo! Finance

"Lisa Horuczi Markus has written a book that makes clear for others all that I know is true:

- That money isn't everything but it is one thing; you too can excel.
- That if you can dream it, you can see it. If you can see it, you can achieve it.
- That money may not bring you happiness, but happiness may bring you money.

I was so thrilled that all of these mantras that I have used and that I have experienced in my life have been placed at your feet. Placed at your feet and bundled in a kit that includes an exercise in possibilities that can change every aspect of your life. Use this book as a guide for perhaps the most exhilarating time of your life. I hope you enjoy this journey. I have."

—John Henry McDonald, CEO/Founder, Austin Asset Management Co.

"An inspirational book that illuminates the connection between spirituality and personal wealth. *Living a Blessed Life* is a book that I will share with my mother, sisters, friends and my nieces as they are learning the important lessons in life."

—Lucia I. Palacios, Executive Director, Orange County Head Start

"An extraordinary book that shows women how strengthening their faith will actually fuel prosperity. Lisa Horuczi Markus gives women hope and gentle counsel for living a life of purpose."

—Reverend Carol Noel Seaman

"*Living a Blessed Life* helps us strip away the clutter so we can focus on achieving genuine wealth. Drawing on real-life stories, anecdotes, and words of wisdom from philosophers, celebrities, theologians, and financial advisors, Lisa lifts us up to understand our own financial genius and live a joyful life."

—Stacy Schaus, PIMCO, Senior Vice President of Defined Contribution Services

"A unique and refreshing blend of life lessons and smart finance."

—Robert Crane, Principal, Intellivest LLC

"Intelligent and insightful. A true standout in the sea of financial books flooding the market. A book not just about money, but a book to read to learn to live a contented and fulfilled life."

—Sid Mittra, PhD, Emeritus Professor of Finance

LIVING A BLESSED LIFE

WALKING IN FAITH, GROWING IN WEALTH

LISA HORUCZI MARKUS

Change One Life
Aliso Viejo, CA

Published by Change One Life
9 Gala Court, Aliso Viejo, CA 92656
www.blessedlife.biz

TO ORDER:

> Online: www.blessedlife.biz
> E-mail: order@blessedlife.biz
> Phone: 949-305-4025
> Mail: Orders
> 9 Gala Court
> Aliso Viejo, CA 92656

> Cover design: Stephanie Snead
> Editor: Joy Parker
> Copy editor: Kathryn Lowe
> Layout: Lisa Sullivan

The opinions and statements published are the responsibility of the author(s), and such opinions and statements do not necessarily represent the policies of Change One Life.

Library of Congress Cataloging-in-Publication Data
Horuczi Markus, Lisa
Living a blessed life: walking in faith, growing in wealth / Lisa Horuczi Markus.
p. cm.
ISBN: 978-0-9790782-0-0
1. Wealth—Spiritual aspects

Printed in the United States of America
First Edition

Footprints in the Sand
Mary Stevenson

One night I dreamed I was walking along the beach with the Lord.
Many scenes from my life flashed across the sky.
In each scene I noticed footprints in the sand.
Sometimes there were two sets of footprints,
other times there were one set of footprints.

This bothered me because I noticed
that during the low periods of my life,
when I was suffering from
anguish, sorrow or defeat,
I could see only one set of footprints.

So I said to the Lord, "You promised me Lord,
that if I followed you, you would walk with me always.
But I have noticed that during the most trying periods of my life
there have only been one set of footprints in the sand.
Why, when I needed you most, you have not been there for me?"

The Lord replied, "The times when you have seen only one
set of footprints in the sand, is when I carried you."

CONTENTS

ACKNOWLEDGMENTS

If books are babies, I've benefited from many midwives. Bob Crane mentored me and shepherded the book through printing and distribution. Joy Parker and Kathryn Lowe provided love, editing, and guidance that moved the book from conception to creation. Stephanie Snead and Lisa Sullivan gave the book life with their graphic design and original art. John Henry McDonald, Kathryn Linehan, Randy Steele, Stacy Schaus, Joline Godfrey and Steve Moeller lent their expertise and input during the development process.

Special thanks to my husband Denis, to my mother Darlene Horuczi, and to the rest of my family and friends for their love, encouragement, and support through the learning process.

FOREWORD

Not long ago, I was asked to meet an amazing woman—a woman who had a passion about sharing all that she had learned in years of school and professional financial management and who wanted to share it all for free. She wanted to build a group of women who were empowered to share what they had learned in their lives, and then help each one of them grow to greater richness. Now this is my kind of woman. And then I was introduced to Lisa Horuczi Markus. We shared ideas, we shared friends, and then she asked me to read her book. "Just give me your comments," she said. But when I read it, not only did it explain what I already felt and knew to be the truth, but much of it I had already begun to implement in some shape or form. As I read more, it began to draw me in on a personal journey—a journey that I had been trying to start on my own for the last three years. As my journal and journey started, I could say, "Yes, I knew that!" or "So *that* is why I have always felt that way!"

But then, as I passed my first week, I began drawing into my life and into my journey the things that had eluded me before. Is it a coincidence that it also was the beginning of the Lenten season (a period of reflection)? I don't think so, because I believe that nothing happens by accident, and instead, God decides that you are just ready for one more piece of your beautiful puzzle that we call "life."

As I looked at *Living a Blessed Life*, not only did I see the beauty and the grace of which Lisa speaks so often, but I could also see how she truly lives her book. Her home is lovely, neither too big nor too small. It is decorated in elegant yet simple tastes. She and Denis fill their home with items that are truly meaningful to them, such as enlarged black-and-white pictures that they took on vacations or of special moments with their children. Her counters are clear of clutter, just as she clears her mind of distractions when she speaks directly to you. It is truly amazing to see that in a day and age of "keeping up with the Joneses" or buying bigger and bigger "just because I can," that there truly are people who hold great values and practice what they preach.

However, when it comes to preaching to you about finance, Lisa and her beautiful book do not. She will not give you all the answers, because that, dear reader, must come from you if you are to finally find yourself on the path to the wealth and richness that you so truly desire. She will guide you and offer support, she will give you references, and then she will give you something to think about. I hope (and know, really) that on the following pages many of you will recognize, perhaps for the first time, your authentic self, stripped of posturing, conceit, emotional armor, and any other defense mechanism that normally obscures your view. Despite our individual uniqueness, most of us are more similar than we are different, and we stumble along in life until we are ready to hear the truth for the first or the hundredth time. I pray that now is *your* time and that you will allow Lisa to be your teacher—because she will put you on your own path to *living a blessed life*.

—Stephanie Nielsen, PharmD
Wishing You Wellness, a Holistic Wellness Center

INTRODUCTION

My mother's childhood was anything but blessed. Darlene Horuczi experienced poverty and economic uncertainty in her childhood. Living in a small, green, asbestos-sided home in Melvindale, Michigan, Darlene was raised to believe that the ticket to security lay in marrying the right man. Her mother told her to find someone with an education and a good job. *He* would be a good provider.

When my mother had saved a year's worth of tuition, she applied at her high school for acceptance to Michigan State University. Her mother called the high school counselor and told the counselor not to process the paperwork. Her mother believed it was a waste of money.

My mother married my father, adhering to her mother's idea of financial security. She suffered many years of physical and mental abuse—like her mother before her. Limited by lack of opportunity, my mother stuck it out in the marriage, stopped the cycle of abuse, and instilled a different belief system in her three daughters:

- You will be financially independent.
- You will never rely on someone else for security.
- You are worth it and you will go to college.

Today, many girls still believe the fairy tale my mother was taught. Joline Godfrey, author of *Raising Financially Fit Kids*, often asks girls how they are going to take care of themselves. Most often, the answer is "marry a rich man."

Cinderella and Snow White could count on Prince Charming, but today's girls can't. According to the Census Bureau, nine out of every ten women will be solely responsible for their own financial well-being. Compared with men, women live seven years longer, earn 25 percent less, and receive 25 to 75 percent less in pension and Social Security benefits. As a result, more than 70 percent of those in poverty are women. That white horse left the stable and left behind it divorce, disappearing pensions, double-digit retiree medical inflation, and an unstable Social Security system.

The Ownership Society

"Since the 1980s, the world has been moving from institutional to personal safety nets," Godfrey said. "Those that don't take responsibility for their financial well-being will be at risk."

During his second inaugural address, President George W. Bush introduced the idea of an "ownership society." He characterized it as a society that values responsibility, liberty, and property. Free from dependence on government handouts (becoming owners instead), individuals are in control of their own lives and destinies. In the ownership society, patients control their own health care, parents control their own children's education, and workers control their own retirement savings.

Striving to be "owners" may sound reasonable on the surface, but it's wrong. The problem with how we approach our financial security is that we think we "own" what we have. We think we've earned it. We think it's ours to do with as we see fit. Bush says we should strive to be "owners." God says we should strive to be good stewards or, in today's vernacular, "managers." The resources we have are *not* ours—they are on loan to us from God. According to 1 Timothy 6:17–18:

> Commend those who are rich in this present world not to be arrogant nor to put their hope in wealth, which is so uncertain, but to put their hope in God, who richly provides us with everything for our enjoyment. Command them to do good, to be rich in good deeds, and to be generous and willing to share.

The world may beckon us to act in a certain way. Whether you label it as being "owners" or "consumers," the messages are pumped out by marketing machines that don't care about the negative repercussions of our behavior. In the midst of so much temptation and so many mixed messages, how do we balance self-preservation with spiritual preservation? I began to ponder this question after the birth of my daughter, Grace. How was she going to learn the most important lessons about managing her finances if I didn't teach her?

Money Problems Have Nothing to Do with Money

In almost twenty years of formal education, never once did I receive a lesson in personal finance. Not in grade school, middle school, high school, college, or graduate school. Like most people, I learned the basics from my parents, and the rest from research and self-study. For the most part, personal finance still is not widely taught in public schools. And wherever financial education *is* taught, it's certainly a separate discussion from faith. Faith never enters into the financial equation—it's saved for conversations about church and charity. Most people don't recognize it as a key ingredient in making *everything* possible, including wealth.

If giving financial planning presentations to thousands of *FORTUNE* 500 employees has taught me anything, it's that money problems have nothing to do with money. This book is a personal journey in the areas of faith and finance to distill what I want my daughter Grace—and women everywhere—to know about real security.

As We Give, So We Receive

One of our greatest needs as humans is to love and be loved. When we enter the world, we are pure love. Children live each moment as if it were the *only* moment—giving love without regard to getting it back. The pure nature of the love they offer is intoxicating for those who are open to receiving it. As a result, children often get back tenfold the love they give so freely.

It's a recognized law of the universe that you get what you give. Maybe what you receive won't look exactly the way you think it will look, but in abundant and surprising ways, you will receive back what you have freely given. If you give love freely, you will be loved in return. If you give peace, you will receive peace. The trick is to give with a full heart—expecting nothing—and to allow the universe to work its magic. This is the essence of faith.

So, what if the same were true for money? What if you lived in an abundant world where money, love, and time were in limitless supply? What if you could create financial security and contentment out of thin air? What if you could live a rich and satisfying life, regardless of how much money you had in the bank?

You can.

This book is about choosing abundance. Regardless of your net worth, the stage you are at in life, or your religious or spiritual belief system, this book offers a simple path to clearing out the underbrush, preparing and fertilizing the ground, and growing your wealth—both inner and outer. The steps are simple but not easy. But if you are willing to invest the time and effort in learning and applying the financial and spiritual tools offered in this book, you will be guided through a remarkable process of self-discovery in several areas.

What This Book Will Teach You

First, this book will help you to identify your *beliefs* about money, enabling you to identify your unconscious financial blind spots and stumbling blocks. You will begin by examining your beliefs about self-worth and why most of us do not feel that we truly *deserve* to live an abundant life.

You will also receive tools to help you stop limiting yourself and learn to expand your perceptions of what's possible. In other words, you will learn how to *dream big*.

One of the most valuable things this book will do for you is to give you four steps for creating abundance. We will examine these steps in detail and teach you how to apply them to your life. I mentioned the first step above: Start with self-worth. The other steps are:

- **Learn four financial habits**—manage your money wisely.
- **Practice contentment**—learn how to live a life of joy and gratitude.
- **Pass it on**—invest in your friends, your family, and the world. Watch your wealth grow in relation to how much you help others.

This book also offers basic advice on how to set financial goals and diversify your investments for the greatest return. Resource lists have been compiled to help you further enrich your spiritual and financial wisdom and well-being.

Finally, this book features a 21-day journal so that you can personalize your journey, identify your life purpose, set goals, and track your progress—creating physical, emotional, mental, spiritual, and financial riches in your life. Studies have shown that it takes 21 days to form a new habit. This journal will take you by the hand and guide you on a journey to understanding yourself and the amazing possibilities life has to offer you.

I know the ideas in this book are sound because during the process of writing it, I myself have grown in faith and have experienced many financial and personal blessings. It's my sincere hope and prayer that you too are blessed as you travel this road.

CHAPTER ONE

LIVING A BLESSED LIFE

At this very moment, you have everything you need to live a blessed life. A blessed life is the joyful existence that God intended for you. It's marked by the fruits of the spirit described in Galatians 5:22–23 (New International Version): "But the fruit of the Spirit is love, joy, peace, patience, kindness, goodness, faithfulness, gentleness and self-control." All this is yours. Love, peace, and joy are within your grasp. They knock at your door and ask to come in. Do you hear? Turn off the television. Silence your cell phone. Log off the computer. Look inside. Listen.

Do you hear it? That voice. The one that says no one should buy a car that costs more than their annual salary. That having eight credit cards is asking for trouble. That getting a new house, boat, television, or purse isn't going to solve what's really bothering you. That planning for retirement is *your* responsibility. That hoarding leaves less for others. That sharing and serving provides more peace of mind than a day at the spa.

That is the voice of your financial genius. Born from a connection to God, it's inside of you. It comes to you in the quiet and it sounds like a whisper. You hear it when you take a moment out of your day to listen. You hear it when you're in a spiritual place—a church, a synagogue, a temple, the forest, the beach, your living room—wherever you invite God's presence.

If you listen to it, you realize that God has provided you with all you need for a rich life. If you ignore it, all the money in the world won't satisfy you.

Financial Hysteria

In our culture, that voice is difficult to hear. "A trickling flow of hysteria pervades our day-to-day mental functioning, constantly influencing our thoughts and emotions," says Marianne Williamson in *Everyday Grace*. Hysteria fuels our fears, clouds our judgment, and shatters our peace of mind. It causes us to doubt ourselves and disconnect from God. It affects the way we deal with people and possessions and has put us on a crash course for financial ruin. Consider this:

- Forty-three percent of baby boomers and 50 percent of Gen Xers will not be able to retire. (Boston College)
- More than 40 percent of U.S. families spend more than they earn. Americans live on 104 percent of what they earn. (Federal Reserve)
- Fifty percent of Americans live paycheck to paycheck and one financial crisis away from bankruptcy. (Dr. Tom Garman, Virginia Tech Professor Emeritus)
- Ninety-six percent of all Americans will retire financially dependent on family, charity, or the government. (U.S. Department of Health & Human Services)
- Almost one out of every one hundred households in the United States will file for bankruptcy. (www.cardweb.com)

- The U.S. personal savings rate is at the lowest point since the Great Depression: 0.5 percent. (Commerce Department)

"Debt has become a part of who we are," said radio talk show host Dave Ramsey. "That spoiled kid in the grocery store. 'I want it. I want it. I deserve it because I breathe air.'"

We live in a land of plenty—plenty of colorful products, clever advertisements, and careless credit—but our lives are overshadowed by fear. No matter how comfortable we are, fear surfaces in familiar forms. In *God's Psychiatry*, Charles L. Allen describes a story of the Allied armies caring for war orphans after World War II. Despite being well-fed and receiving excellent care, the orphans slept poorly. A psychologist solved the problem by putting the children to bed holding a piece of bread. By clutching an "edible" security blanket, the children knew they had food for the next day and could sleep.

For most of us, that "piece of bread" is money. Like war orphans, most of us live in fear of not having enough of it—to make the rent, to provide for our families, to keep up appearances. We mistakenly think that money can satisfy our deepest needs. We mistakenly make money the goal—not the means to *achieving* the goal. We become embroiled in the endless cycle of more: the more we want, the more we get, the less we are satisfied, the more we want.

What we truly crave is what money can never satisfy—connection to God.

Our financial state is a reflection of our inner search and struggle for this connection. It's a superficial sign of the state of our soul. Like peeling back the layers of an onion, what on the surface appears to be a financial problem actually has a physical/material source. Peel back the physical problem and we uncover a mental source. Peel back the mental problem and we uncover an emotional source. Peel back the emotional problem and we uncover the spiritual root of all the other problems.

The financial, physical, mental, and emotional states are impermanent. They change day to day depending on the state of our soul. Our soul is our immortal essence. According to Genesis 2:7, it is the breath of God that made lifeless dust a "living being." Think of the soul as a sound and think of the fiscal, physical, mental, and emotional states as the echo of that sound. An echo does not sound different from its source—it is a faint audio replication of the original sound.

Consider a woman who repeatedly declares bankruptcy. She has a good job. She's smart and attractive. How is it that she always ends up broke? Even when she comes into a financial windfall, it evaporates into clothes, jet skis, vacations, bills, repossessions, and foreclosures. On the surface, you might say she needs debt counseling or a financial planner. But financial literacy and planning only treat the symptoms. She spends for emotional reasons: she wants to feel better about herself, find her soul mate, transcend her life. Spiritually, she's bankrupt. Earning more doesn't matter. Her real craving is for love and connection.

This story plays out again and again everywhere in the world every day.

The source of all financial problems is spiritual poverty. That's why financial education alone often fails. It works like prescription drugs—it treats the symptoms, but it doesn't cure the patient. Our needs were meant to be satisfied by our Maker, not by money and what it can buy.

Spiritual Connection

Seeking a spiritual connection has been humankind's quest throughout time. St. Augustine tried to fill himself up with wealth, wisdom, women, and worldly pursuits until he found his truth in Christianity in 387 AD. In 534 BC, Sidhartha left his princely life to pursue enlightenment that became the path of Buddhism. Muhammad desired connection with one God, Allah, and founded Islam. Seeking connection is our deepest craving. "There is a desire within each of us, in the deep center of ourselves that we call the heart," writes Gerald May, Senior Fellow in Contemplative Theology and Psychology at Shalem Institute for Spiritual Formation. "We are born with it, it is never completely satisfied, and it never dies. We are often unaware of it, but the desire is always awake."

Today, we're searching for an immediate, transcendent experience of God. A September 2005 *Newsweek*/Beliefnet Poll found that 79 percent of Americans, especially those younger than age sixty, described themselves as "spiritual." Nearly two-thirds of Americans said they pray every day, and nearly a third meditate.

Although our soul desires connection, it's difficult to stay centered in this self-centered, me-first world. The world says we should seek pleasure—do whatever feels good. *It's okay if you don't go to church. Just pray when you get around to it.* The world says we deserve possessions—the one who has the most toys wins. *How can I make more money to buy more things?* The world says we should strive for independence and power—take control! *I made this money. I'll spend it how I want.* The world says we should strive to be popular—do whatever it takes to be liked. *To be liked, I need to wear the right things, drive the right car, and live in the right neighborhood.*

In the world's framework, God is sandwiched between yoga and pedicures and is called on as a personal genie to grant our wishes. As in Wilbur Reese's poem "$3 Worth of God," we become morally bankrupt when we think of God as a commodity for purchase:

I would like to buy $3 worth of God, please.
Not enough to explode my soul or disturb my sleep,
but just enough to equal a cup of warm milk or
a snooze in the sunshine.
I don't want enough of him to make me love a black man
or pick beets with a migrant.
I want ecstasy, not transformation.
I want the warmth of the womb, not a new birth.
I want about a pound of the eternal in a paper sack.
I'd like to buy $3 worth of God, please.

Living a rich life means turning away from what the world thinks and toward what our soul knows. It means realigning our idea of wealth and security with what really matters. It means getting back to basics—you and God.

Real Security

Often we define our identity and purpose by external results. Life defines us. In a never-ending quest for love and acceptance, we allow externally driven events and approval of others to determine our state of being. We are success. We are failure. We are popular. We are lonely. We are wealthy. We are impoverished. We are whatever we are experiencing or achieving at that very moment. Our life, like a fragile leaf, is floating and falling, blown about by things outside our control. We do not control the actions and reactions of others any more than we control the weather. Connection with God is unattainable in this type of existence. It will not come to the conflicted mind.

But we don't have to live like this. Our life experiences do *not* define us. Real security comes from reliance on God for all our needs and desires, large and small. True wealth is found in our relationship with God. Without our connection to God, we eventually run dry because we were not designed to live a disconnected life. In Genesis 22:14, God is referred to as "Jehovah-jireh," which means "the Lord will provide." The Bible contains more than seven thousand promises of this true provision. By living in faith, we enrich our lives.

Financial security rests in a personal connection to God, being accountable for our actions, and living each day focused on fulfilling the call that God has placed on our life and, therefore, on making the world a better place. Aligned with God's love and peace, we find true prosperity and fulfillment. Psalm 46:1–3; 10–11 (New International Version) says "God is our refuge and strength, an ever-present help in trouble. Therefore we will not fear, though the earth give way and the mountains fall into the heart of the sea, though its waters roar and foam and the mountains quake with their surging…Be still, and know that I am God; I will be exalted among the nations, I will be exalted in the earth. The Lord Almighty is with us; the God of Jacob is our fortress."

God helps us in time of need. As depicted in Psalm 23, we see that He is our Shepherd and we "shall not be in want." People who seek God's purpose find that their ideas of wealth are realigned in unexpected ways. As prosperity flows *to us*, it then flows *through us* to bless the lives of others. For example, have you ever given money to a charity and then received a raise or a break on your taxes that more than made up the amount you gave away? What we give, we truly receive. This *true* wealth not only increases our level of contentment, but also redirects us in ways that will bring glory to God. When we live in faith, the abundant life of the Fruit of the Spirit (Galatians 5:22–23) becomes evident: love, joy, peace, patience, kindness, goodness, faithfulness, gentleness, self-control.

Bruce Wilkinson, author of *The Prayer of Jabez*, always carries cash. He loves to talk to people about their life dreams and then make their dreams happen by giving and encouraging others to give. One memorable story of his generosity describes a corporate meeting during which one of his managers shared that his vision was to complete his master's degree. "What's stopping you?" inquired Bruce. The man said money. Bruce then reached into his wallet, pulled out all the cash he had, gave it to the man, and invited everyone else at the meeting to do the same. He did so, expecting nothing in return and fully believing in God's abundance. Bruce is richly blessed—financially and spiritually—because he is willing to give both money and spiritual support unconditionally. He makes himself a vessel to bless others. Cash and kindness flow through him.

By aligning with God's purpose, we are guaranteed a good result. Romans 8:28 reminds us: "And we know that in all things God works for the good of those who love him, who have been called according to his purpose." When problems and obstacles arise (as they always do), we know that God will help us work through them and help us handle them in a fiscally responsible way.

Real Genius

You have financial genius within you. Don't laugh. It's true. Your current financial situation, comfort level with investing, level of education, and past track record with money do not measure the true level of your financial genius. Financial genius is not defined by your investment picks, the school you graduated from, your current address, or your last name.

The word *genius* has a lot of baggage—as does the word *financial*. Let's unpack the myths so we can tap into our *true* financial genius.

Myth 1:

Genius has to do with IQ.

Genius is one of the most misused words in the dictionary. Today, it is shorthand for someone with an IQ of 140 or more. But that is not the origin of the word. With our culture's emphasis on the superficial, we have lost the multifaceted meaning of genius.

In ancient Roman mythology, the "genius" was the guiding or "tutelary" spirit of a person. Everyone was considered to possess inner genius, according to Thomas Armstrong, Ph.D., *Seven Kinds of Smart*. Genius was regarded as a guardian spirit that follows a person through life and helps her overcome obstacles. Today, that genius is known as "that still small voice"— something we can access through prayer and meditation.

Research shows that we begin learning in the womb and that this learning continues throughout life. Every person has the capacity for limitless learning—making each of us potential geniuses. Author Elbert Hubbard said that "Genius is only the power of making continuous efforts." We determine our level of genius by our vision, intention, and actions. Genius is nurtured when we can discern our unique calling and purpose— and act on that knowledge.

Most of us live life by accident rather than by intention. Our lives, goals, wants, needs, standards, and dreams are dictated by external factors such as the media, an employer, our family, etc. We become so consumed with living that we forget who or what we're living for.

We are called to genius by God. It's our responsibility to express our innate brilliance because it honors our higher power and it gives others permission to shine too. Matthew 5:14–16 illustrates God's pleasure when we begin to dream big and tap into our genius: "You are the light of the world. A city on a hill cannot be hidden. Neither do people light a lamp and put it under a bowl. Instead they put it on its stand, and it gives light to everyone in the house. In the same way, let your light shine before men, that they may see your good deeds and praise your Father in heaven."

Marianne Williamson mirrors what we just read from the Gospel of Matthew. She identifies what keeps us paralyzed in mediocrity as the fear of our own brilliance—the fear of success. In *A Return to Love*, she says:

> Our deepest fear is not that we are inadequate. Our deepest fear is that we are powerful beyond measure. It is our light, not our darkness that most frightens us. We ask ourselves, Who am I to be brilliant, gorgeous, talented, fabulous? Actually, who are you *not* to be? You are a child of God. Your playing small does not serve the world. There is nothing enlightened about shrinking so that other people won't feel insecure around you. We are all meant to shine, as children do. We were born to make manifest the glory of God that is within us. It is not just in some of us; it is in everyone. And as we let our own light shine, we unconsciously give other people permission to do the same. As we are liberated from our own fear, our presence automatically liberates others.

> So the real question is not, Who are we to be geniuses?— but, Who are we not to remember that we are, indeed, children of God?

I often speak to mothers' groups about what it takes to raise a financial genius. Most expect that the talk will focus on helping children understand the value of money and will offer tips on handling allowances. They are surprised to find that the focus is on how *they* handle money, and the messages this sends to their children.

As young children, we're born into a conversation of scarcity that teaches us that love, money, and time are in short supply.

But they are not. If you divided all the money in the world among its inhabitants, everyone would have $1.2 million. And time is a human-made measuring stick. If something is important enough to us, we *make* the time for it. Time is like love: We create love, and the more we love, the more love there is. So, finding your financial genius is accomplished by creating a conversation of abundance and then acting and growing from that belief system.

Consider Tina who is in the process of teaching her daughter Katie to tithe. Tina helps Katie stuff the offering envelope with quarters and talks about how many people will be touched by her daughter's gift. She takes her daughter out of the nursery to put the envelope into the offering plate as a physical demonstration of the act of giving. When Tina volunteers at homeless shelters, Katie goes along with her to see her gift of time at work. Tina not only serves as a role model for Katie, but also reinforces her own beliefs by sharing them with her daughter.

Genius is a natural inclination given to us by God to guide us through life. It's the marvelous opportunity within each of us to live a fuller life. There are financial rewards to following our genius, and financial consequences to ignoring it. I recently asked a coworker for a charitable contribution to Head Start, an organization that focuses on empowering children and parents by providing them with access to education and health care. She said she already was passionate about another charity and that any dollars she gave should go to it. Her scarcity mentality was revealed in the belief that what she gave to Head Start would not be replenished—that if she gave away five dollars, it would disappear and she would never get it back.

But what would it be like if she believed that whatever she gave would come back to her tenfold? What would be possible for her? I can clearly imagine her receiving not only money, but also love, trust, and joy as she opened herself up to greater blessings.

We can know abundance of life or we can dwell in spiritual poverty—it is our choice.

Myth 2:
Personal finance is boring and beyond me.

There is nothing boring about personal finance. Knowing and living a few simple financial truths can liberate you. It can give you freedom.

Go to any bookstore, online or on foot, and you'll be amazed at the number of books on the topic of financial planning. One thing most of those books have in common is that they make financial planning much more complicated than it needs to be. Handling money is not rocket science.

Managing your personal finances is just like attaining your proper body weight—success boils down to understanding a few key principles. Maintaining healthy body weight is knowing to eat the right foods in moderation and enjoying regular exercise. Balancing your personal financial life is learning to spend less than you make and investing that money to make more.

Oscar Wilde once said, "Anyone who lives within their means suffers from a lack of imagination." Nothing could be further from the truth. It's impossible to live within your means unless you have a clear picture of the future, big dreams of a better use for your resources, and a willingness to ask God for guidance.

Myth 3:
Wealth has to do with luck and/or intelligence.

According to Webmath.com, a third of Americans think the only way they can achieve financial security is to win the lottery. They believe wealth has to do with luck. Others think that financial security rests on your level of intelligence, your family name (if it's a famous one), or having an excessive amount of money.

But true wealth stems from how you feel about yourself, your Maker, and your future. Author Lillian Eichler Watson said, "If the principles of contentment are not within us, no material success, no pleasures or possessions, can make us happy." Think about all of the wealthy (and not so wealthy) people who are unhappy and seem to follow one frivolous pursuit after another. Think of the lottery winners and the common story of their downfall after their windfall. Think of any *True Hollywood Story*: person is poor, person finds fame and fortune, person hits bottom or dies after adopting a party-hard lifestyle.

Living an abundant life has nothing to do with money—it has everything to do with contentment. In Thom Hartmann's book *The Last Hours of Ancient Sunlight,* there is a chapter called "The Secret of Enough," which explodes the myth that the more money we have, the happier we will be. Hartmann shares a story of his wife's grandmother who survived the Great Depression on the family farm by growing the family's food herself, burning wood, making her family's clothing, and recycling/reusing everything she could. Now in her nineties, this remarkable woman has enough money from investments and the sale of the farm to live as extravagantly as she pleases. Yet she doesn't because she knows that joy is found in simple living, not in things. "She still buys her two dresses each year from the Sears catalog, collects rainwater to wash her beautiful long hair, writes poetry, and finds joy in preparing her own meals from scratch." Hartmann points out that unlike others who were so psychologically scarred by the Depression that they blindly embraced the myth that more things equal greater happiness, she understands that money cannot buy spiritual peace of mind.

Connection to God, living a life of purpose, and being grateful for what you have is financial genius. It comes from the conviction that at each given moment, God has given you exactly what you need to live your best life. That doesn't mean you don't work toward a brighter future. In fact, your conviction drives you to work harder because you have a purpose. It isn't an excuse to give up. It's an opportunity to look up and let yourself be guided to something greater.

Claim Your Riches

Financial education and help have never been more accessible, including tens of thousands of Web sites, thousands of books, and hundreds of credit counseling services. We hear about the importance of weaving our own safety net, how health costs may eat up 5 to 20 percent of our retirement income, and that Social Security may not be around. Still, most families live one financial crisis away from bankruptcy and haven't adequately saved for the future. Personal bankruptcies and credit card debt have skyrocketed to all-time highs, while personal savings rates, 401(k) plan participation, and retirement plan balances have plummeted to all-time lows. According to Virginia Tech University's professor emeritus Dr. E. Thomas Garman, forty million Americans are overly indebted or financially stressed—and it's affecting their jobs, their health, and their lives.

If we're financial geniuses, why are so many of us on our way to the poorhouse? Because our bottom line has more to do with our belief system than our bank account—and we're all spiritually bankrupt. All security—physical, emotional, and financial—rests in our day-to-day connection to God. We can read all the financial books in the world, make the best stock purchases, live in a mansion, and drive a Ferrari; yet, if we don't know God, we are broken and may not even be aware of what we are missing.

Fundamentally, we crave a connection to our Maker. We want to know that our life means something—that our net worth is no measure of our self-worth. We need reassurance that if we leap off this world's treadmill—which is fueled by fear, debt, and work—we will land in a better place. That once we stop the guilt purchases, the spending sprees, and the competitive acquisitions to "keep up appearances," we will still be loved, we will still matter, and we will still exist. We also need to refresh ourselves on and follow some commonsense financial habits to increase and responsibly use our financial resources.

But it's hard to take a leap of faith when Madison Avenue has its crosshairs on your forehead. Billions of advertising dollars morph into messages expressly designed to separate you from your dollars. Credit is today's opium of the people: You want. You buy. Don't have the cash? Don't worry. Someone stands ready to give you an infusion.

Do you believe there's a better way to live? You bet there is! Grace is more than the period of time you have to make your credit card payment.

Want to start living a rich life beyond your wildest dreams? Trust in God—not MasterCard, not the media, not Warren Buffet.

The path is simple, but not easy. Reconnection with your financial genius can be accomplished in four steps, which I write about in great detail in chapters two to five:

Step 1. Start with self-worth. Your value is not based on your bank account. Your net worth is not your self-worth. Everyone has financial genius. Tap into your financial genius by finding your life purpose.

Step 2. Learn four financial habits. Wealth doesn't happen by accident. To live richly, you must be a good manager and adopt these four financial habits:

— Spend less than you earn

— Systematically save

— Spread your risk

— Share with others

Step 3. Practice contentment. A minister once summarized the beatitudes in one sentence: "God loves you, now act like it." You have everything you need to live a life of joy. Live simply. Love more than you spend. Adopt an attitude of gratitude. Your wealth grows with your level of contentment.

Step 4. Pass it on. Make a difference through your daily actions. Invest in your family, friends, community, and world. Your wealth grows in relation to how much you help others.

Prayers and Blessings

I pray that you will find a message in this book that puts you on the path to spiritual and personal wealth. Spiritual wealth builds personal wealth. Spiritual wealth allows you to live with purpose, appreciate God's blessings in your life, and enjoy every moment. It focuses your energy. You work hard for a purpose and are blessed. When you are spiritually affluent, you see your wealth as a resource on loan from God to make the world a better place. Your purpose influences how you handle your money. It boosts your immunity to becoming greedy. It equips you to invest in what matters.

Relying on God doesn't absolve you from following the laws of wealth. If you're lazy, if you don't save, if you squander your savings, if you invest foolishly, if you think that someone else is to blame for your financial situation, or if you otherwise misuse your resources, you're going to have a rough life. Frederick Douglass, a former slave, once said, "I prayed for 20 years and received nothing until I prayed with my feet." You still need to work hard and respect and use money correctly. Spiritual wealth feeds financial wealth. Faith helps you to be of value to others and earn money. Faith also guides your good stewardship of this income to use your resources to bring glory to God through making the world a better place. In Matthew 25:31–40, Jesus proclaimed, "Blessed are those who care for the hungry, sick and homeless." In Acts 20:35, we learn that "it is more blessed to give than to receive."

God created the world with a thought. Before creating the world, God *imagined* what man and woman would be like, what animals would roam, what plants would grow, what every part of the planet would look, smell, taste, sound, and feel like. If humankind is created in God's image, we also create our world through our thoughts. Our perception influences our level of prosperity. What we think of ourselves determines whether we *attract* wealth or *repel* it. If you think of yourself as impoverished, that is what you will become. If you think of yourself as a vessel for God, being constantly filled and overflowing, that is what you will become.

As an example, let's look at the life of a woman who constantly proclaims "I can't afford it." With this belief system in full force, she effectively shuts down opportunities for creating the money to afford what she wants, because, in effect, she is telling the universe "No, don't give me any extra wealth." Most likely, she *will* notice more and more the things that she can't afford, and she will attract hardships to herself—such as sickness, car repairs, divorce—that will put her more firmly on the path to poverty.

However, if this woman were to say "I'm *open* to the possibility of creating more wealth"—and genuinely set this as her intention—everything in her life would shift. She would begin to notice and act on opportunities to improve her financial situation; for example, getting a new job that pays more than she's making now. She would attract good fortune, such as receiving an unexpected tax return, discovering that the cost of something she really wanted is less than she expected, or finding/manifesting a mentor to help her better handle her money.

"Every time you state what you want or believe, you're the first to hear it," said Oprah Winfrey. "It's a message to both you and others about what you think is possible. Don't put a ceiling on yourself."

God gives us freedom to choose our thoughts and actions, but in order to make the most of this tremendous gift, we must be aware of the belief system that we are allowing to shape our world. Each one of us can make a choice to make our lives easy or difficult by our thoughts and our interpretation of events. We can choose the type of daily mindfulness that creates a heaven on earth, or we can choose attitudes and interpretations of events that can make each day a living hell. Shifting our internal conversation to considerations of things that will have eternal significance for us—loving God and living our lives in service to God, loving our neighbors as ourselves, helping others—will cause our financial situations to shift as well.

Consider Rick Warren, senior pastor of Saddleback Church in Lake Forest, California. When Warren was in seminary, he prayed about where he should start a church, and he was called to Orange County, California. Guided by that vision, he packed up his family into a station wagon and drove West. No money. No place to live. He pulled off at the first real estate office he saw and stated his mission. "I'm Rick Warren. I'm here to start a church. I need a place to stay." The agent offered Warren his condo rent-free for three months. Warren asked him if he attended a church. He said no. Rick said, "You're my first member." That real estate agent is still a member of Saddleback Church. Over the past twenty-five years, Warren has been fulfilling his call, which includes writing the bestseller *The Purpose Driven Life*. Saddleback Church has grown to more than twenty thousand members, and this abundance has overflowed from Rick's life so much that he reverse-tithes. Yes, he lives on 10 percent of what he earns!

Think about your own life. Have you ever sensed the connection to God our creator, the very source of all creation, and found your resources replenished? Synchronicity? Coincidence? Perhaps this is God deciding to remain anonymous, waiting for you to realize His power and point it out to others.

In Acts 1:8, the Bible states, "You will receive power when the Holy Spirit comes on you; and you will be my witnesses in Jerusalem and to the ends of the earth." Realize that in the power of the Holy Spirit, you can be a witness of Jesus' life-giving abundance that will change each life you touch for the better—by the way you think, the way you live, the way you handle money. Like Rick, once you start to create your life from the spiritual realm, you will start thinking, feeling, and using your time and resources in a new manner. Money will never be the same in your hands. It becomes a resource to make significant positive changes in the world.

This book is meant to serve as a road map to a healthier, more spiritual connection with prosperity and contentment. As you read it, I hope your heart will be touched and you will see how you can be a more effective steward of your financial resources. Ready to find your financial genius?

Chapter Two

Start with Self-Worth

At the core of Western religious and philosophical belief is the intrinsic value of life. Every life has value. Every life has a purpose. Unfortunately, most of us underestimate our own value and are unclear about why we're here on the planet. We buy into popular culture's definition of worth—that you are what you do and what you own. The world says your value will be measured exclusively in relation to what others have. This limits you to a life of frustration and failure because there will always be someone who has more than you. Believing in the world's value system ties you to a treadmill of endless work to prove your worth. Now is the time to redefine yourself and how you measure wealth.

Net worth is not self-worth.

You are a unique creation—so valuable that no accountant could calculate it. Like an original work of art, there is no other like you. Irreplaceable. Valuable beyond all measure. You.

Knowing your value and believing your incredible worth is the baseline for a healthy relationship with money. Without a strong definition of self-worth, money is meaningless. There is nothing you can measure your self-worth against.

God loves you. You were created in God's image. Your worth springs from these facts. Nothing you do will diminish God's love for you. Nothing you do (or buy) will increase your value in God's eyes. God is already crazy in love with and devoted to you.

How you handle money is ultimately an expression of self-worth. If you know and believe you are worth something, you will live richly at any income level. If you think you are worthless or if you doubt your value or are confused about your purpose on this planet, you will use money in damaging ways to fill the void. Your needs will be insatiable. The more you spend or abuse money, the more worthless you will feel.

Feeling worthless is a self-inflicted wound stemming from our comparing mind. We are continually calculating our value in reference to what our sister, neighbor, coworker, or favorite celebrity has. In the *Wall Street Journal* article "The Secret to a Happier Retirement: Friends, Neighbors and a Fixed Annuity," Jonathan Clements states that people have a more pleasant retirement if they account for their "comparing mind" as well as their bank accounts. He said to pick your neighbors as carefully as you invest your savings, because measuring your success against your neighbors doesn't ever retire. So if you can't afford to keep up appearances living a block from Rodeo Drive in Beverly Hills, consider retiring to rural Montana.

"Instead of moving to a neighborhood you can barely afford, you might go somewhere that you can comfortably afford," said Erzo F.P. Luttmer, an economics professor at Harvard University. "That way, you'll be among people who are taking the less ritzy cruises, and you will be more content."

Said another way, H.L. Mencken's definition of wealth is income that is one hundred dollars a year more than his wife's sister's husband.

Constant comparison erodes self-worth because there will always be someone wealthier than you. Someone more beautiful, intelligent, witty, stylish, thoughtful, compassionate, articulate, fortunate, creative, fertile, or anything else you seek to be. That craving to be something different from what you are fuels reckless spending to disguise your perceived deficiencies, to buy friends, or to keep up appearances.

If you think this way, change your mind. If your tendency is to compare yourself to others and feel that you're always coming up short, start counting your blessings. If you're feeling blue, volunteer at a homeless shelter, nursing home, or orphanage. There is always someone out there who has it worse than you and needs your help.

Shortly after a friend of mine moved from a bohemian New York City neighborhood to affluent, upscale Orange County in Southern California, she began to feel that maybe she didn't measure up. Everyone she met seemed to have a bigger home, a better car, and a more materialistic lifestyle than she had. Soon she began feeling bad about herself. She received a big reality adjustment, however, when she traveled to rural Latin America on a writing/research trip and later began helping her hometown branch of the coworkers of Mother Teresa to distribute food to needy families. Suddenly she realized that she enjoyed a hundred times more material comfort, prosperity, and blessings than the great majority of the world's people. She clearly saw how ridiculous she had been to feel "less than" and began to gratefully count her blessings, giving thanks for her good and blessed life.

Lose Your Price Tag

In *Rich Dad, Poor Dad*, Robert Kiyosaki describes an important turning point he experienced when given the opportunity either to accept a high wage for a job he hated or to fully realize his own power to create wealth from a job he loved. He and a friend had apprenticed themselves to "rich dad," a self-made, successful entrepreneur, so that they could learn his secrets for making money. "Rich dad" talked them into working for him for free to see how long it would take the boys to get fed up with that arrangement. After several weeks, the boys finally announced they were fed up. "Rich dad" bought them each an ice-cream cone from the store where they worked and sat them down on a bench. "Rich dad" started offering them increasing sums of money to see what it would take to keep them working at a job they hated.

At first, the boys' heads were spinning at the thought of such large sums of money. Then Robert caught on to the game: "Rich dad" wanted to see if they had a price, if he could keep them working at a job they hated by throwing more money at them. As a result, Robert and the other boy began to think more creatively about their work situation and how they could create opportunities to earn more money while having fun. One thing they noticed was that the store manager would tear the covers off the comic books that didn't sell and give these covers back to the distributor for credit. She then would throw away the rest of the comic books. The boys brokered a deal with the store manager and the distributor to collect the comic books instead of seeing them thrown away, and they created a library room in the basement where children from the neighborhood would "rent" the comic books for a small fee. The boys employed one of their sisters to be the librarian and paid her part of what they earned. The boys made lots of money and had fun in the process.

According to Kiyosaki, most people are caught up in the "greed-fear" trap. They see things they want and buy, buy, buy. They get in debt. They are fearful of losing their jobs and not being able to make their bills. They work, work, work to pay those bills. And just as they get close to paying things off—greed comes back into play, beckoning them to buy more.

The root cause of all bad financial decisions is fear. If you're not living up to your potential, if you're stuck in a job you hate, if life isn't turning out the way you planned, it's because of decisions you made based on fear.

If you believe you're a beloved child of God, you can never be bought. You will come to a place where money has no power over you. A place where you are in control—unswayed by the siren song of possessions. A place where you step lightly and with purpose on the earth.

You get to that place by strengthening your faith in God. There is no shortcut. Think about Mother Teresa. She had an incredible impact on the lives of Calcutta's poorest of the poor. By the end of her life, she was so highly acclaimed that she could have lived anywhere, in any manner she chose. However, she continued to live life simply. She had few clothes, one set of eating utensils, and one set of bed linens. Mother Teresa was never swayed by the wealth and flash she came in contact with. Instead, she stayed focused on her original mission of empowering the poor. Her focus on this goal was so pure that she wouldn't even keep extra rubber bands. She gave them away.

Know You Are Worthy

"In every aspect of our lives, we are always asking ourselves, How am I of value? What is my worth? Yet I believe that worthiness is our birthright."

—Oprah Winfrey

To know your worth is to know your destiny. You were put on this earth to do great things, large and small. Each day, you have the choice to allow yourself to be governed by fear or faith. It's your decision. Your beliefs influence your thoughts. If you think you are unworthy, you will procrastinate in all matters, including wealth. By putting off doing things that would be good for you, you will justify your belief that you are worthless. However, if you choose to believe you are worthy, your thoughts will reinforce your value and you will create wealth. You can change your life at any time by noticing what you are thinking, identifying the underlying belief that triggered the thought, and replacing the belief with something more empowering. Walking in faith gives you the power and perspective to change.

It takes faith to see yourself valuable and whole as God sees you. Faith in God is the ability to maintain a positive mental attitude when everything else in your life seems to be falling apart. John Henry McDonald credits his success to his unshakeable faith. Now the CEO of Austin Asset Management, as a child, McDonald ran away from home four times. One of the good memories of his childhood was living with his uncle and learning the value of having a positive mental attitude (PMA). He learned it so well that he earned the nickname "little giant" from the insurance salesmen at his uncle's company. The six-year-old in suspenders used to swagger into his uncle's office and proclaim, "My PMA is terrific." Despite dropping out of school, being drafted into the Vietnam War, and going broke three times, McDonald is a multimillionaire today because of PMA and a strong belief in God. He has formalized the discipline of living in faith through structured visualizations called "Exercises in Possibilities."

"It's like structured dreaming," says McDonald. "Each year, I take 21 days and think about every aspect of my life—spiritual, emotional, mental, physical and fiscal—and I think about what I want to create. I put down how much I want to earn, what I want my relationship with [my wife] Louise to be like, how I want to serve my clients, what I want my relationship to be with God, what I want my legacy in the community and world to be. I don't leave anything out and I think big. I have been doing this for years and I still have my journals from all those years. In my first journal, I wrote myself a check for more than $70,000, well over anything I had made previous, and I cleared $65 over the amount I wrote down.

"I don't talk about it much with my clients because no one asks about it. But it's made me a millionaire many times over. My spiritual growth has increased my business growth year after year. I could quit work today and have an annual salary of $200,000 a year. Some might call this 'magical thinking.' I don't care what you call it—faith, magic, malarkey. But it works."

In fact, McDonald's fifteen employees voluntarily engage in visualization for ten to twenty days a year. They meet each holiday and share their visions of what they hope to achieve spiritually, emotionally, mentally, physically, and fiscally.

"The only thing that keeps us from achieving anything we set our minds to is fear," McDonald says. "From this day forward, you are not allowed to worry. There is a beginning to every worrisome thought and when you feel it coming on, say to yourself, 'No, I won't worry.' Doing this alone will change your life."

Find Your Purpose

Worry stems from lack of faith. One of the best ways to improve your faith is to find your purpose.

According to Rick Warren, the search for purpose has puzzled people for thousands of years because we start at the wrong place—ourselves. We read self-help books and question our choice of spouse, career, house, food, geographic location, hobby, and bottled water. We think that picking up a serving from our guru de jour will change our lives. Instead, we end up missing our greater purpose, and end up serving only ourselves—instead of others—and suffering for it.

According to Buddhist teachings, every sentient being has the right to be free from suffering. The goal of life is to be happy. However, the more you buy in to the notion that you are what you wear, what you drive, where you live, and what you own, the more you enslave yourself to suffering. Your life soon belongs to someone else or to some institution as you work to pay off bills that keep piling higher and higher—bringing you no closer to your destiny.

My mother always told me never to love anything that couldn't love you back. Her words recently came to mind as I went to buy an outfit for my daughter. A cute little shirt caught my eye with the saying "I love shoes" in curly, girly script along with the image of a dozen different shoe styles. It was adorable without a doubt. But I got hung up on the words I was putting in my daughter's mouth if I bought her the shirt. I know my daughter loves milk. I can't say for sure that she loves shoes. What if she grew up to be another Imelda Marcos with thousands of pairs of shoes? What if she found herself on a psychiatrist's couch and it came out that her obsession with shoes could be traced back to a shirt her mother bought for her when she was nine months old? What if she came to prize shoes more than people?

Why isn't there a shirt with the smiling faces of children from around the world that says "I love people"?

Decide What's Worth It

In December 2005, my mother gave me a clipping from *The Detroit Free Press* that said "There is an imbalance in the ratio of time and effort to results. Instead of pushing for more, go the opposite way. Accept less or none, then you'll have the space to consider what actions are their own reward."

Profound? I don't know. But I liked it enough to write it down in my journal. Quite frankly, I didn't know what to make of the statement. I couldn't figure out what it meant. Every so often, I'd take it out, ponder it, and put it back.

It wasn't until months later that I got a sense of its meaning while working on a culture video at Western Asset Management (WAMCo). From Pasadena, California, came one of the most amazing companies I'd ever encountered. A fixed-income management company, WAMCo was neither the sexiest in its industry nor the most commanding. But this soft-spoken company continually attracted unique employees: surfers, mountain bikers, marathon runners, and Hawaiian singers who, by the way, all knew bonds inside and out. This was especially unusual in a business that was known for its blue suits, mahogany-paneled offices, and big egos. But these employees were as passionate about their personal pastimes as they were about their professions, giving them a unique sense of balance.

What was so unique here? What ultimately made this company stand out as really special? It hit me when we were videotaping CEO Jim Hirschmann: We set up the shot at WAMCo's main entrance. I had expected to have to reshoot several times because of road noise or wind. I wasn't expecting that our primary source of interruption would be whistling

WAMCo employees. They weren't doing it to ruin the video. They didn't even know we were there, but stumbled upon us unexpectedly. Embarrassed, they would apologize and continue into the building. And each time we'd chuckle. Nice problem to have that your people are so happy they whistle at work.

Which brings me back to the newspaper clipping. Hirschmann said that he would work for WAMCo even if they didn't pay him. Maybe you could dismiss this as an enthusiastic CEO who is so well off he doesn't need to work; however, he wasn't the only one saying this. Throughout the ranks, the words rolled out: "I'd work here for nothing...I'd work here if they didn't pay me...As long as they'll have me, I'm going to work here."

What causes someone to want to work for free? Don't they have bills? Don't they care about getting ahead? If you were to think about life as an equation, you might get this:

$$\frac{\textbf{Time}}{\textbf{Effort}} = \textbf{Results}$$

In the case of WAMCo employees, they were willing to work for the company regardless of whether their efforts translated into financial gain for themselves. In return for their time and effort, they were receiving something greater than money. There was something about the place that physically nourished them— an atmosphere of camaraderie and mutual respect. There was something that mentally engaged them—ignited their curiosity, challenged them intellectually. There was something emotional—people were getting choked up when they talked about the company, their clients and their coworkers, what WAMCo stood for, and how proud they were to be a part of it. And there was something spiritual—the place pulsed with purposeful people building something fun and worthwhile, creating something better than your average bond company.

Just like Robert Kiyosaki and his friend, WAMCo employees were financially liberated by doing what they loved. They had become rich doing something they would have done for free.

What would happen if you did the same? What kind of work do you love to do? What is your vision for your life? What truly brings you joy? If you believed you had the choice, what type of work would you do just for the fun of it? How would your life be transformed if work was no longer work, but a way of living and loving God? What is the price of working at a job you hate, one that sucks the life out of you? Why is that paycheck worth so much, and your life and happiness worth so little? It's time to start valuing yourself more than money. The starting point is being specific about what you want in your life—spiritually, emotionally, mentally, physically, and fiscally. If you focus only on the things you don't want, that is what you will draw to yourself. Take out a blank sheet of paper and invest in yourself by thinking about and writing down what truly will make you happy.

Five Fields of Endeavor

As mentioned in the introduction, we've been given five fields of endeavor to dream in: spiritual, emotional, mental, physical, and fiscal. Our spiritual endeavors are core and they're the foundation for all the other fields. The spirit is the only 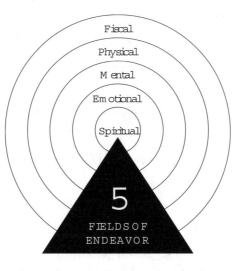 part of us that's eternal and it's the portal through which we experience all things. The rest of the fields are impermanent, and the further removed from the spirit they are, the more superficial they become.

Your fiscal field of endeavor is the by-product of your spiritual, emotional, mental, and physical endeavors. The stronger your spiritual, emotional, mental, and physical states, the richer your life will be. Your fiscal state will improve as you invest in the other areas.

As you grow in spirit, you'll enrich your emotional state. You'll feel more balanced and have a more positive perspective. Your ability to give and receive love will increase. As you open emotionally, your mental state will become more optimistic. You'll see opportunities that weren't visible through your old lens. I call this letting "Polaroid vision" overtake you. Do you remember Polaroid pictures—the instant pictures that came out of the camera blurry but sharpened their focus after moments of exposure to the air? When you open yourself up to the possibilities of life, what was once blurry becomes clear, like a Polaroid picture. The magnifying power of a positive mental attitude will bring new sharpened perspective to your life.

As you expect to see positive forces at work in your life, they will magically appear. You'll realize that those forces were there all along, but now you are finally able to perceive and appreciate them. Fueled by a vastly improved mental state, your physical state will perk up and follow suit. Energy will infuse you as you purposefully pursue your vision.

It's only after you work through these fields that your fiscal state will become as healthy as the rest of you. And as riches befall you, you won't even care about them because they will pale in comparison to what you've experienced spiritually, emotionally, mentally, and physically. You'll gladly invest your wealth in whatever will bring to the rest of the world the love, peace, and gratitude you feel.

Think about Bono from one of the world's most beloved rock groups, U2. The man has more money than God, but he wears the same clothes day in and day out and often forgets to shower. He is constantly on the move, taking a stand for a resolution to the AIDS epidemic, encouraging governments to forgive the debt of Third World countries and give humankind an opportunity to flourish. He doesn't rest and he rarely sees his family. He is a man on a mission. And the more of his personal fortune he gives to his causes, the more he receives in return. His cup truly "runneth over" because he gives so fearlessly.

Live in abundance by building your spirit. Give what you want to receive—love, money, time. Like a boomerang, it will come back to you. Hit you in the head. And be careful what you give. Don't invest energy in fearing your pursuits—your fear will grow. It takes faith to put yourself out there in a positive way. When you truly live for good, regardless of the reward, you'll receive your reward abundantly. There's no cap on the amount of love, success, peace, prosperity, and happiness in the world. They grow with compound interest. Each begets itself.

If changing your perspectives and creating a healthier spiritual attitude toward wealth seems like an overwhelming task, remember that this book includes a 21-day journal/workbook to help you identify the attitudes and habits that don't serve you and to enable you to form new habits. Working through this journal will help you clarify your life's purpose, set attainable goals, learn how to dream big, and focus your energy.

Exploring the Five Fields of Endeavor with Your 21-Day Journal

Your journey to true wealth has to be from the inside out. And be forewarned, the path is simple, but not easy. All the money in the world isn't going to satisfy you if money is all you want.

Money won't make you safe, keep you warm at night, calm your fears, or nurse you back to health. In the right hands, it is currency to change the world. Until you're spiritually healthy, money may come and go, but it won't stay and grow.

It takes 21 days to form a habit. And learning how to respectfully handle money is one of the best habits you can adopt. To learn how, you need to start with your soul. To evaluate what really matters in life, you first need to write it down. The act of writing not only expresses your intention, but it also sends a clear message to your source power—that strong, sure voice of guidance—that you are in need of assistance.

Invest the time in yourself to nourish yourself spiritually, emotionally, mentally, physically, and fiscally by journaling your dreams, desires, fears, aspirations, and intentions. Cut out pictures. Doodle. Talk and write in bold colors. Do what feels right to you and keep with it for 21 days. Do it on your own or use the journal in the second half of this book to guide your journey. Only *you* can drive the bus. So let's get on with it. Time is precious.

Three Steps to Improve Your Self-Worth

Here are some ideas to help you realize your self-worth:

1. **Read *The Purpose Driven Life* by Rick Warren.** Take an inner pilgrimage to find your purpose. This book is broken down into daily digestible wisdom to help you meet your destiny. When you zero in on how you fit into the bigger picture, it's easier to handle your resources with wisdom and restraint.

2. **Make decisions that reaffirm your worth.** Dr. Phil says that people make life decisions and daily decisions. Life decisions have to do with what you value. Are you

living in a way that brings you joy? Daily decisions reinforce your life decisions—you're either digging yourself in deeper to a life that you loath or you're building a stairway to heaven. It's your choice. Make a list of your life decisions—what's most important to you, what you want people to say about you after you've passed on. How do you want to live your life? If you choose a life of integrity and purpose, your daily money decisions need to reinforce that direction.

For example, a woman I know longed to explore foreign diplomacy and to make a difference in the lives of others. As a starting point, she decided to become involved with Wheels for Humanity, a global humanitarian organization that provides the handicapped with sports wheelchairs and medical support. To her delight, she discovered that the more she volunteered, the more that possibilities opened up for her to live her dream of making a difference on a global scale. As her vision became clearer, she began to use her money with purpose, giving freely where it was needed, trusting it would be replenished, and investing wisely.

3. **Give thanks for your resources.** Most of us live by the belief that the glass is half empty. To reframe your life, start thanking God for the glass and whatever is in it. It doesn't matter how much money you make, how many toys you own, what you drive, what excuses you use, who you know, how many friends you have, who left you, how old you are, what you look like, or if you have shoes. It doesn't matter. There will always be someone worse off than you are. Pray for that person. Be thankful for what you have and what you don't have. God uses us for a greater

good, no matter what our perceived weaknesses. When you start to be thankful, you start to feel powerful. You start to take control of your financial future.

This can happen in big and small ways. For example, a woman named Michelle would often go to the mall with her cousin who would always press her to buy things she didn't need. On one trip, her cousin was goading her to buy a hip pink purse. "Buy it. You know you want it." Michelle asserted her power by withholding her plastic. "Yes, I could buy it, but why? I have better things to do with my money than to buy something I don't need."

Always remember that you are a magnificent creation. In a culture that constantly reminds us of what's missing in our lives, it's difficult to keep a perspective of our self-worth if we go it alone. Creating a closer relationship with God reaffirms our eternal value. The more you seek God, the less you'll spend.

CHAPTER THREE

LEARN FOUR FINANCIAL HABITS

*"If you know peace, then you thrive; if you know contentment, then
you are rich."*

—*Zen Lessons: The Art of Leadership* by Su Shi

The way you handle wealth glorifies God. And in order to handle
wealth, you need to master a few core financial habits. These
habits have a specific financial cause and effect for everyone, just
like the law of gravity has a specific effect on all objects.

Most Americans live on 104 percent of what they earn.
When you consistently spend more than you earn, it's impossible
to get ahead. You can pray about it. You can consult your rabbi,
priest, pastor, or astrologer. You can play the lottery or bet on a
horse. You can get a handout or a temporary fix. But if you
don't learn to live within your means, you won't get ahead. You
simply need to spend less than you earn in order to have anything
to save and invest.

And as you reduce your appetite for stuff and start to save,
a curious thing happens. As your balance grows, so does the
balance in your life. Your self-confidence rises along with your

sense of contentment. As you learn to live on less, you enjoy life more. Stripping away the clutter allows you to focus on what really matters—your time and the people you want to spend it with.

There's no shortage of financial education gurus, Web sites, resources, and books. In fact, there's so much available and so many complex and conflicting messages, you may be wondering where you should start. Essentially, financial success boils down to adopting four core habits:

- Spend less than you earn
- Systematically save
- Spread your risk
- Share with others

No matter how much faith you have, if you don't practice these habits, your money won't last. As Cardinal Francis Spellman once said, we need to "Pray as if everything depended on God, and work as if everything depended upon man."

1. SPEND LESS THAN YOU EARN

"It all comes down to this. If you are going to accumulate enough assets to make a difference in your life, you must spend less than you earn."

—*The Average Family's Guide to Financial Freedom*
by Bill and Mary Toohey

The cardinal rule of wealth accumulation is *spend less than you earn*. It's the core lesson of *The Richest Man in Babylon* by George S. Clason. Most of us operate under the illusion that all of what we earn is ours and that we can do with it what we want. That we are in total control. But we're not. In actuality, everyone gets a cut except us. Taxes come out of our paycheck, whether we want them to or not. Most of us pay a portion of our earnings for health insurance. We need to buy food, maintain our cars, pay rent or a mortgage, and clothe ourselves and our children. We pay the preschool, soccer league, grocery store, landlord or bank, dry cleaner, and gas company. It should be easy to live within our means, but it's not.

When I was twelve, I wanted a horse. We lived in a suburb of Detroit. Automotive factories, power plants, and strip malls dotted the landscape—not pastures, barns, and farm animals. Each weekend, my parents drove forty miles each way to drop me off at a riding stable where I cleaned stalls, groomed horses, and led trail rides. During my first year of working there, I negotiated a deal with the owner to buy Misty Blue, a fourteen-year-old, white, one-quarter Arabian (three-quarters close to the glue factory). Coincidentally, the asking price was exactly what I had saved in quarters—$350. It took me a year of delivering newspapers, babysitting, passing out flyers, selling seashells, getting gift money, washing cars, and cutting lawns to save that amount. I didn't give one thought to the ongoing cost of owning a horse, which was easily more than $350 a month. Thankfully, my parents put the brakes on the deal before it went through; otherwise, I'd still be trying to pay off the debt of owning that animal.

Media Assault

Wouldn't it be nice if we all had a benevolent third party to save us from getting in over our heads? Instead, there is a nonstop, continuous stream of advertising aimed right *at* our head. On our way to work, we're hit by radio ads, billboards, and advertising-wrapped buses. At work, we encounter Internet pop-up ads, solicitors, telemarketers, and school fundraisers. At home, we can't escape television, newspaper and magazine ads, catalogs, more telemarketers, neighbors' testimonials about the new miracle products, and pleas from our children to get what Johnny's got. The only time we're safe is when we're asleep—but that might not even be the case, because our minds may replay our kids' requests for a certain toy or we may have nagging thoughts that we've run out of laundry detergent.

Even at the beach, there's no escape from advertising. Most weekends, my family and I spend time at Laguna Beach in California. And every weekend, you can count on a couple of planes flying banners to advertise the latest movie, cell phone company, or restaurant. Wouldn't surprise me to soon see some clever marketer harness the poor dolphins with a pop-up ad that becomes visible each time they surface.

What is the net effect of all this advertising? We stop listening to ourselves. We stop trusting God. We forget our financial genius. Instead, we buy in to the idea that we need to drive the biggest SUV, live in a McMansion, dress in the latest fashion, and eat steak or sushi every night.

Since when did a mani/pedi, a daily Starbucks, or an Evian water become a necessity? Since we digested a steady diet of nonstop advertising—one that costs us dearly. According to Juliet Schor, author of *The Overspent American,* each hour of television we watch increases our spending by $208 a year. Ouch.

Immediate Gratification

We easily fall victim to the siren's song of advertisers because we're wired for immediate gratification. Our lower brain (prelimbic system) lights up like a pinball machine when we make a purchase. We not only *love* spending money, we get *high* on it. No wonder so many people use shopping as a form of therapy. Whether you're bored, lonely, angry, depressed, happy, or fearful, shopping is only a car ride or a click away and always ready to accept your credit card.

Another reason it's so easy to spend is that our whole economy is set up to disembody the purchasing process. Turn back the clock twenty years and remember a time when you wanted to buy an outfit. You drove thirty minutes to your favorite store and spent an hour picking out the perfect outfit. After fifteen minutes in line, you paid cash for it. On the drive home, you thought of the three other black outfits you had that looked just like the one you bought. Did you really need it? Maybe you turned around and returned it. You got that cold hard cash back in your pocket and felt smart about not buying something you didn't need.

Today, that same decision process takes you fifteen minutes on the Internet instead of two hours at the mall. You use a credit card, so you don't have the visceral effect of parting with physical money. Using the credit card puts distance between you and what you've earned. It also gives you the illusion that you're not spending your paycheck, because your bank account hasn't changed and your wallet hasn't become lighter at the moment of purchase. The purchase is completed so quickly, you have no time to reconsider your decision. Lightning-quick processing squeezes out buyer's remorse.

Recently, a coworker mentioned a book to me. During our five-minute conversation, I pulled up the Amazon.com Web site, found a used copy of the book (which had been out of print for a decade), and used Speedy Checkout to cement the deal. The book was bought before we hung up. I don't recall the name of the book and I'm sure it's probably something I didn't truly need, but the streamlined purchase process allowed my enthusiasm to override my logic.

Spend Wisely

The way we spend money determines our financial destiny. We spend every day. At most, we may save only each pay period.

And how we spend money largely depends on how we feel about ourselves. Mother Teresa of Calcutta once remarked that loneliness is the poverty of the West. She said, "We think sometimes that poverty is only being hungry, naked, and homeless. The poverty of being unwanted, unloved, and uncared for is the greatest poverty. We must start in our own homes to remedy this kind of poverty."

To spend money wisely, watch how you spend your time. Your greatest resource is time—not money. Care enough about yourself to spend some time each day nourishing your soul. Slow down and talk to your spouse, your children, and your friends. Paint. Knit. Read. Walk. Pray. Play. Love. Find something that replenishes you. Do it daily.

You don't have time? Do it anyway. "If you're important enough, they'll wait," said John Travolta in *Be Cool*. You *are* important enough. They will wait. Put your playtime on your list of things to do. Check it off after you've done it. Do it daily.

In her book *Everyday Grace,* Marianne Williamson suggests starting each day by lighting a candle and spending some quiet time in prayer and meditation. Having two children under the age of three, I read this line in her book and laughed out loud. I barely find time to go to the bathroom, let alone find undisturbed blocks of time for meditation. But I began to pray about finding the time to start my days this way. The time miraculously materialized—sometimes at 4 a.m., sometimes at 7 a.m., sometimes at 2 a.m. Now each day reveals a couple of moments I can light that candle, thank God for the blessings in my life, bless those that I will come in contact with that day—people I know, those I have yet to meet, and those I will never know—and ask God for direction on how I can be of best use that day.

When I take time to do this, I find that my life becomes simple. My relationships are more harmonious. I get more enjoyment out of work. Everything flows, and even when it doesn't, I'm better able to cope.

Create Awareness

Money has energy. God has power. If you want to change your spending habits, pray for God to show you a greater use for your money. When I first saw the Sarah McLachlan video *World on Fire*, I sobbed. It starts with McLachlan sitting on a chair in the middle of a modest room, playing the guitar. The viewer is asked, "What's wrong with this video?" It's revealed that it cost $1,500 to make instead of the usual $150,000. The video shows what happens when she donates the difference to charities around the world. For example, instead of spending $5,000 on hair and makeup, McLachlan put 145 girls in Afghanistan through one year of school. To give the audience an idea of how far an American dollar can go in the developing nations of the world, you're introduced to a single mother in Ghana, Africa, who works two jobs, sixteen hours a day, to earn $200 a year to send her son to school. She needs to sell fifty oranges to earn one dollar.

One of many powerful lyrics in the song is "The more we take, the less we become. The fortune of one man means less for some."

How are you using your wealth? Sometimes we get trapped in our own view of reality—that Detroit, Las Vegas, or New York is the center of the universe. Our desire for a newer car, a bigger boat, a larger home takes precedence over any greater good we could do with our money, like planning for retirement, saving for our children's college education, or keeping people from starving. We choose where we focus our awareness, how we prioritize our needs and wants, when and if we open our hearts to others, and how we spend our money. The question is, What are you spending your money on and what is it worth to you?

As part of Pastor Rick Warren's P.E.A.C.E. Plan (described at www.saddlebackfamily.org), he gave a sermon at Saddleback Church about the causes of poverty and why we should care about it. Most people end up assuming that people are in poverty because they are lazy. In reality, most live in poverty because of culture, circumstances, calamities, and corruption. Saddleback's plan for eradicating poverty focuses on giving people opportunity—not giving a person a fish, or even teaching them how to fish, like in the old adage, but teaching them how to *sell* a fish. One line from the sermon stuck out for me:

"Are you willing to live simply so that others can simply live?"

How are you living? What meaning does money have for you? Is what you're spending your money on really worth it?

The Magic Standard

When I was five years old, I had a favorite shirt that I would have worn every day to school if my mom had let me. Faded flannel with fawns frolicking over it, it was mauve, it was mine, and I loved that shirt. I wish I could recapture that magical feeling with any article of clothing I have now. Alas, they are just clothes. But just think how much less you'd buy if you held your purchases up to that "magic" standard: Is this shirt something I would want to wear more than one day in a row? Will it turn me into a princess? Will it make me feel cozy and safe? Am I willing to give away some of my other clothes to make room for it in my closet?

Hold this same awareness for every purchase you make. Hold it up to your own "magic" standard. I'll bet you buy less.

The World's Most Simple Budget

I can't claim credit for this idea. Denis, my husband, came up with it when we decided to cut our credit card spending in half. He said, "We're not the type to fill out a spreadsheet each time we buy something. Why don't we just set a limit and track our spending on a whiteboard. If we spend under the limit, we get to keep the difference as a splurge."

We've been using the whiteboard idea ever since. The limit applies only to the credit card. We write the dollar amounts we spend on the board and total them at the end of the month. It works for us. It might work for you.

Some expenses are fixed and you can't do much about them: your mortgage or rent, your car payment, your utilities. But some expenses are variable and you *can* control them: entertainment, eating out, cell phone, cable, gizmos and gadgets for yourself and the kids, etc. Decide what your spending should be—make that decision independent of what you are spending now.

Pay in cash. Studies show that using cash instead of a credit card cuts your spending by 18 percent. That's because money is money—it has energy. Pay attention the next time you hold a dollar. What does it feel like? What does it look like? Flip it over. Look at both sides. Run your fingers over George Washington's wig. What does a dollar mean to you? Would you throw it away and burn it? Do you feel the same when you hold a $50 or $100 bill? Do your hands get a bit stickier?

How about your credit card? Hold it. Do you feel the same energy? Do you feel the same way about it as if you were holding a dollar?

How about converting your cash into a purchase, such as Thai food? Put some pad Thai in your palm. Do you feel any energy? Does it feel or look like $5? Do you value it the same as a $5 bill? Food is easier to throw away than a $5 bill. When money is converted into an item, it's easy to lose track of the original value.

One of my most favorite Suze Orman sayings is, "To get in touch with your money, touch your money." If you want to curb your expenses, don't use a credit card—pay in cash.

Keep Yourself Out of Harm's Way

Target stores tempt me to the limit. Whenever I'm in one, I spend more than I planned. The shelves are stocked with such well-designed, reasonably priced stuff that I lose it—and my money. Whether it's toilet paper or tops for the kids, Target is my weakness. What's yours?

If you want to stay sober, you stay out of bars. If you want to keep within a budget, you stay out of stores—the ones made of bricks and mortar and the ones online. Find something else to do.

Stuck on something you want to buy but know you don't need? It plays over and over in your head. You keep visiting the Web site, doing the research, working the numbers. Are you running out of willpower and excuses not to buy it? Pray. You are never in this alone. Ask God for guidance on how to use your money. You'll see a path that probably doesn't include another pair of shoes.

Cancel your subscription to fashion magazines. Don't open the catalogs that are sent to you. Turn off the television. Boycott the media. Don't worry about missing out on world events. If it's a big enough story, you won't be able to hide from it, no matter how hard you try.

If it were my decision alone, I'd get rid of our television and banish Bob the Builder into oblivion. Part of this has to do with seeing Bob once too often over the last three years. Part of this has to do with me *not* wanting my kids to think that a size two is normal, that it's cool to kill people, or that your life's problems will be solved by buying The Clapper. There are some intelligent programs on television and I would miss them, but when I stack them up against the danger of allowing others to dictate what's important and what I should focus on, it's not worth it to me. I don't have the energy or the emotional surplus to spend worrying about television characters. And since I've become a mother, I can't stand those crime shows about missing children nor do I want to think about a world in which that kind of stuff happens. What's the use of feeling scared and depressed? I'd rather use my energy to spend time with my family and work to make the world a better place instead of watching it whirl out of control on television.

A dear friend of mine, Roberta (Bert) Urbani, put her television into the closet when she enrolled her son Gabe at the Waldorf School in Detroit. At the time, she was a single working mother, and putting away the television allowed her to make every moment count with her son. It took discipline to cut the television viewing back to almost nothing, but the payoff was an increased family connection and less cost and demand for the toys and food products advertised on television.

Establish a Support System

A support system, even if it is only one dedicated friend, is extremely helpful when transforming your relationship with needless spending. As a recovering Target shopper, part of my therapy includes walking (and I don't mean down the aisles of the store). My friend Michele and I meet most Sundays after church to take an hour walk around the neighborhood or in the local canyon. The walking is good not only for my heart, but also for my soul. I put Gracie in her BabyBjörn baby carrier— she likes to be part of the conversation—and we walk and talk until we're too tired to do either. Each walk saves me about $100—the average of what I usually spend at the store.

My friend Stephanie doesn't spend a moment at the mall— she'd rather paddle with her crew in competitions along the beaches of California and around the world. She puts her energy into doing something she loves and additionally raises money through charity events for her other passion, environmental nonprofits. Staying out of the mall saves her $500 a month.

My coworkers Mike and his wife Julie have come up with their own answer to the gas crisis. They stay healthy and save at least $45 a week in fuel costs by biking to work together each day. Instead of paying a high price at the pump, their only cost is pedal power plus sweat, resulting in stronger bodies and uninterrupted together time on the way to the office.

Friends can be great allies in your fight to spend less. Find yours. If you don't have any, make some by participating in an activity you like. Or get a dog, a cat, or another pet. Pets can be great companions and wonderful listeners, and dogs like to go for long walks on the beach. Surround yourself with supporters.

Do Something Positive

As much of a charge as you might get out of buying something, you'll get an even bigger charge out of changing something for the better. If you want to feel better about yourself, help someone else. You'll feel the shock waves all the way to your soul.

Each Christmas, my friend Roberta (Bert), whom I mentioned earlier in conjunction with putting away the TV, used to organize a caroling visit to her mother's nursing home. Bert brought the song sheets and cookies—the rest of us brought our voices. Long before the caroling was scheduled to start, the residents would make their way to the community room. We'd chat with them and do some crafts while waiting for everyone to arrive. Bert always brought construction paper, scissors, tape, and her previous year's Christmas cards for anyone who wanted to create decorations. You'd think we were doing the residents a favor, but really they were doing *us* a favor: They allowed us to share our time and whatever talents we had. They willingly and appreciatively received what we offered. As we all sang together, the sickness and depression that might have been there the moment before were forgotten. Faces transformed—showing a glimpse of what they must have looked like twenty years earlier.

Ever feel powerless to stop spending? Doing something positive is the antidote to powerlessness. Don't get caught up in the what. It doesn't really matter *what* you do, but how much love you put into whatever you do.

Hewitt Associates' mission statement is "To make the world a better place to work." In associate focus groups, some people gravitated to the statement and others wrestled with the idea that they, in and of themselves, could make the world a better place to work. One woman shared her doubts: "I write benefits communication, so how could I be making the world better? The tag line sounds pretty inspirational—like curing cancer." I felt saddened that this woman wasn't convinced of her self-worth and the fact that she could be making the world a better place just by being herself and taking a stand for what she believed in through the way she performed her work. If she were willing to shift her belief, she could empower not only herself, but also everyone else whose life she touched.

Changing the world has more to do with your thoughts than your current actions. To change the world, change your mind. Your thoughts influence your actions.

According to the Buddhist practice of tonglen—a Mahayana meditation/visualization practice—you *can* change the world through your thoughts. The practice consists of visualizing (as you inhale) that you are taking the world's pain and suffering out of circulation and replacing it (as you exhale) with good health and fortune. It doesn't matter if you are a paraplegic in Calcutta or a supermodel in Chicago—you not only have the *ability* to make a difference in the world, but you also have the *obligation*. By doing something positive, you'll fulfill your world obligation and material possessions won't mean as much. Filled with a deeper satisfaction that money can't buy, you'll spend differently—directed by an internal value system. As you live on purpose, you'll spend on purpose and find that you're satisfied with less stuff.

2. SYSTEMATICALLY SAVE

"Whatever you do, or dream you can, begin it. Boldness has genius, power and magic in it. Begin it now."
   —Goethe

As part of Dr. Stephen Covey's September 2005 address to the Financial Planning Association in San Diego, he showed a thought-provoking video to help the audience focus on beginning a project with the end already in mind. It began with a blank canvas and put you behind the paintbrush as the artist. *Imagine your life as a painting—what would it look like? Would it be a landscape, a still life, a portrait? What would be at the center of it—yourself, your family, your possessions?*

Covey's video urged the audience not to live life by accident. Often, we don't see our lives as our own creation, but as the product of circumstances beyond our control. Many take the path of least resistance and are dissatisfied with the result.

Experience a Savings Makeover

To survive, you need to spend less than you earn. To fulfill your destiny, you need to save. Saving has the bad reputation as the ugly stepsister of spending. But don't believe the bad press—**saving is beautiful**. Instead ask, Who's spreading the rumors? Advertisers portray spending as hip and generous. *Express yourself by what you wear, what you drive, and what you drink. Don't think about the cost—you're worth it. Spend more on your children because it will increase their intelligence and happiness—they're worth it.*

Conversely, saving is portrayed as uncool, unimaginative, and unpopular. Don't believe the press! Marketers spend billions to plant seeds of self-doubt that part you from your hard-earned money. They don't care about your dreams of financial independence or about your being able to afford college for your children or about your secure retirement. *They want your money.*

Saving is a heroic act. It says to the world, I have a dream and I'm willing to invest in it. It says to the world, I have a plan and I'm working to achieve it. It says, I have a vision of what I want my future to be and I'm putting my money where my mouth is.

Saving should be celebrated, not vilified. It should be shouted from the rooftops, not muffled or silenced. Spending does *not* make you powerful—any fool with a credit card can buy just about anything. It takes much more restraint and strength to save. *Savers* should be praised—*not* the big spenders.

Saving Is Magic

Anyone can become a millionaire. Saving five dollars a day for forty years and investing it in an S&P 500 index fund will give you around $1 million. Make your own magic by saving.

Here's what the marketers don't want you to know: saving is magic. Once you start saving, you'll notice a difference in your attitude. Positive energy will infuse you. Your gait will become more bouncy. Your head will become filled with possibilities. All you have to do is wave your wand and "poof"—things will start happening for you.

Want this magic, too? Follow this recipe:

- Envision your destiny
- Let your DNA help you
- Channel that energy

Envision Your Destiny

Most of us aren't raised to think we have a destiny. But we do. To find yours, you'll need to retrace some steps of your childhood. "As children, we are seldom told we have a place in this life that is uniquely ours," said author Julie Cameron in *The Vein of Gold: A Journey to Your Creative Heart*. "Instead, we're encouraged to believe that our life should somehow fulfill the expectations of others…rather than being taught to ask ourselves who we are, we are schooled to ask others."

In order to have the courage to save and the conviction to keep it up, you need to define your destiny. What do you want for yourself, for your family, for the world? Think. Give yourself the space to ponder these questions. Don't rush the answer. Pray for the answer. Don't let others dictate what this should be. This is *your* dream. Dream it. Your 21-day journal will give you all the support you need to embark on this journey of destiny; it will give you tools to create an action plan to embrace the amazing purpose for which you were created.

Once you have discovered a purpose for saving your money instead of spending it on things you and your family really don't need, the magic begins. You'll find it easy to put the money away. You'll find resources where there weren't any before. God will open doors to you that previously were shut. Ask for the assistance and guidance to get a clear vision of what you want to achieve.

For example, a woman named Stephanie had a son who was sick with allergies. She took him from doctor to doctor, looking for an answer, but nothing seemed to work. Finally, she was inspired through prayer and meditation to turn to research into alternative and complementary therapies. To her amazement, she began to see results in her son from these treatments. She was so thrilled with the fruits of her research that she felt called to share the gift of thinking-outside-the-box medicine with others and invested in the dream of becoming a holistic pharmacist. Whatever money she spent on her studies to achieve this dream has been more than returned to her by the long list of patients who want her healing counsel. As she uses her gifts to help others, Stephanie's love and wealth continue to grow in endless supply. Her dream continues to grow in the world and she is an inspiration to everyone with whom she comes in contact.

Creating the future we want by honoring our dreams is a more powerful idea than we can ever imagine. John Henry McDonald created the headquarters of his company, Austin Asset Management, in his journal long before he stepped into the physical offices. He cut out images he wanted to see through his conference room window. He found images of the exact office furniture he wanted, right down to the materials from which it was constructed. He drew the image of a modern, streamlined building before he ever saw it. McDonald wasn't at all surprised when a real estate agent took him to an office building that looked exactly like the one he had created in his journal.

"If you can dream it, you can see it and if you can see it, you can do it," said McDonald.

Dream big and quantify it. Put a dollar amount to your dream. Find out how much you need to retire. Find out how much you need for the down payment and mortgage for that home. Find out how much it costs to send your child to school. You don't need to know the amount to the exact penny. In your mind, start painting the picture of your destiny. See it in detail. Journal it. Cut it out. Color it. Feel the texture. Make it real and rotate it around to see it from different angles.

Let Your DNA Help You

You breathe life into your dreams by putting money away for them on a regular basis. And wouldn't you know—God has hardwired us to save effectively. You might be laughing to yourself: *Lisa, you haven't seen my bank account or credit card statement. I'm a hardwired spending machine. Saving is not in my DNA.* But saving is something we were born to do and there's a quirk in human nature that allows us to do it effectively: behavioral finance researchers call it "mental accounting."

Mental accounting is the human tendency to compartmentalize financial decisions. Simply stated, when people set aside money for one purpose, they don't easily use it for another purpose. Researchers say that people who engage in mental accounting don't see the financial "big picture" and subsequently make decisions that aren't the best use of their overall resources. But where saving is concerned, we can use this quirk to our advantage.

According to Columbia University researcher Ran Kivetz, we treat resources differently, depending on how they are labeled or grouped. For example, if you save in a 401(k) plan for retirement, you are less likely to take the money out for a spending spree than if that money was in your regular bank account. That's because you have earmarked that money for retirement—you've assigned a "mental account" for it.

Use all the resources available to save in a systematic way. If your company offers a 401(k) plan, use it to save for retirement. John Henry McDonald, described earlier as the man who literally "dreamed" his office building into existence, called the 401(k) plan "the greatest wealth accumulation vehicle of all time." Sign up and your savings are automatically deducted from your paycheck (pretax). You don't have to think about it. And most companies match a portion of what their employees put away. That's an automatic return on your investment! If you're not already signed up for your company's 401(k), *do so now*. Contribute the maximum amount you can. It's a great way to put away a boatload of money for your retirement. And because your money is in a 401(k) plan instead of at the local bank, you're more likely to leave it alone until retirement.

For your other goals, earmark savings for those goals and save for them in separate accounts. This will help you keep on track with achieving your goals and you'll be less likely to touch the money for other purposes.

My husband and I practice this religiously. We have separate accounts for bills, business, and big dreams. Because we put the money in separate accounts, we empower it for that particular purpose. For example, every penny I've spent to create and promote this book comes from my business account. That is my money to create a legacy of financial empowerment, and I spend that money with the intention of lifting people to the level of their own financial genius. When I write a check from that account, I thank God and experience joy because of what's possible in creating this product. If I change just one person's life, every penny I have spent will be worth it.

Channel That Energy

An object that's in motion stays in motion. An object that's at rest stays at rest. These are some of the most basic laws of physics. When you save, you put your dreams in motion. You start living the life that God intended you to live. Feel that positive energy. Use it to make the world a better place by your daily actions. This will be easy because you'll feel like doing it. It will be natural. As you feel more centered, you'll be able to share your alignment with others.

Others will sense this change in your attitude and altitude. You'll begin to look different, act different, be different. At first this will be subtle—little changes in what you say and do, but all leading toward a seismic shift in how you view the world. Some people may even begin to ask you what's different about you. Answer them honestly. Share your hope with them. Show them that there is another way to live. Let them know that they don't need to be a slave to their possessions, their job, or someone else's world view—that they too can realize their dreams. Everyone is entitled to live their dreams. Set an example that others can follow, and shine a path for them.

My sister Amy was a stay-at-home mother for ten years. Then she made the decision to return to school to achieve her dream of providing her family with financial freedom by becoming a physician's assistant. With her daughters Emily and Macy in grade school, Amy carries a full-time class load at night and volunteers at the hospital while the girls are in school. While she is in school, time and money are tight, but Amy believes in the abundance of God and pursues her goal with clear intention. She even aced her first chemistry test. By pursuing her dreams, Amy empowers everyone to seize the moment and live life to the fullest. Go, Amy!

3. SPREAD YOUR RISK

"When you play it too safe, you're taking the biggest risk of your life...time is the only wealth we're given."
—*I Could Do Anything If I Only Knew What It Was*
by Barbara Sher

On a trip to Paris, I collided with a three-hundred-pound French woman outside the Notre Dame cathedral. It was my fault. I was looking at my map or my eyes were adjusting to the light as I emerged from the dim, candlelit cathedral. My foot crossed her path and she stumbled for what seemed like an eternity until she landed flat on her back—baguettes everywhere.

Call it what you will, but don't put all your baguettes in one basket. We all need to spread our risk. If we put all our money in one place—the stock market, real estate, under our mattress—we're asking for trouble. We're asking for someone to trip us.

Spend less than you earn to ensure your survival. Systematically save to enable you to encounter your destiny. Spread your risk to ensure that your dreams become reality.

What's Diversification?

Life is full of risks. Getting out of bed, driving a car, meeting new people or clients, presenting new ideas at work—all carry some risk. Normally, we don't think that long and hard about the risks; if we did, we wouldn't be able to function. However, there are some risks that loom larger in our minds, take up more space, and seem more dangerous than they need to. Flying in an airplane and investing in the stock market fall into this category of exaggerated risks. The lifetime odds of dying in a plane crash are 1 in 5,704 (the lifetime odds of dying in a car accident are 1 in 228, according to the National Safety Council). And if you ask investors, they will tell you that the chances of a market crash in any given year are 1 in 2. But the experts, such as The Vanguard Center for Investment Research, will tell you that the real likelihood of a crash is 1 in 50.

Diversification is a way to handle risk. Your mom called it "not putting all your eggs in one basket," but it was made famous in Harry Markowitz's 1952 doctoral thesis. In fact, Markowitz went on to win the Nobel Peace Prize for his ideas and work in this area.

Diversification is also how we *intuitively* handle risk. Behavioral finance research refers to this as "1/n behavior." When an investor has a number of investment fund choices and doesn't know what to do, the investor will put an equal amount in each, thus spreading the risk.

I witnessed my three-year-old doing the same thing. He receives a weekly allowance of three dollars in quarters. He can put the money into three containers labeled "Spend," "Save," and "Give." Each time he receives an allowance, we talk about the three choices and then he's free to make his choices. After one of our allowance discussions, I left him alone to make his choices while I unloaded the dryer. When I came back, he had an equal line of quarters in front of each container. To my knowledge, he hasn't read anything on behavioral finance and it's not something I've discussed with him, but he knows how to spread risk.

Where Were You During the Crash of 1987?

October 14, 1987, marks one of the worst stock market crashes in history. The market lost 508 points in a single day. John Henry McDonald, CEO of Austin Asset Management and one of *Worth* magazine's top financial planners in the nation, lived through it, and as a result, it changed his entire investing philosophy and made him an evangelist for diversification. Here are his reflections on that transformation.

I was a newly-minted registered investment advisor, making a living by advising clients to time the market. The kind of advice, as a matter of fact, that many salesmen give today. Picking the hottest mutual funds and guessing the best time to invest is **not** diversification. It's not even very good investment advice.

Anyway, on that day my assistant peeked into the offices and signaled me over with a wave and a smile. "Channel 36 is here to interview you, JH. They're here now."

Channel 36? What do they want? I marched downstairs and glanced at the TV—the market was plummeting! The worst crash in the history of the stock market was happening during my interview.

Channel 36: "What do you tell investors now, Mr. McDonald? Where should our viewers be parking their money?"

I remember now that I prattled on about bonds, and cash, and God knows what. But somehow I avoided the very real answer, "I've no earthly idea where money should be." I've no earthly idea how you should react to a market that is handing out greater losses than any losses, including 1929. And furthermore, nobody else in America has any clear idea of what's happening, either.

October 1987 was a watershed event in my life. As a guest speaker that December at a broker's conference, I had written a presentation about market timing using mutual

fund families. A real "how to" for the broker community.
I ripped it up.

With pen in hand, I sat down and reflected on my experience. As the market plummeted, I had the real feeling that no one had predicted the greatest downturn in stock market history. No one!

So if I'm in the business of consulting, and I truly don't know what the stock market is going to do, what advice can I give about investing?

- **There are different asset classes.** Well, that's true.
- **Some asset classes will do better than others over any given period of time.** Yeah, that works. Works every time, as a matter of fact.
- **Diversification spreads the risk of investing.**

What Is Risk?

From a financial perspective, there are two types of risk: not having enough money (inflation risk) and losing what money you've got (market risk). To reach your destiny, you need to balance these two risks.

Inflation Risk

On a subzero Michigan winter day in January 1991, I found myself in an overheated conference room at the Novi Hilton in northwest Detroit, competing in the final rounds for a world travel grant. I was twenty-two, had never been on a plane—much less out of the country—and only spoke English. My competition was the J.Crew crew—nine preppy, clean-cut, multilingual guys in blue suits and brown loafers. Fluent in

French, Danish, Spanish, and Italian, the Ivy Leaguers talked among themselves about what each was going to do after winning the grant. What I remember most was their beautiful leather shoes, because I spent most of my time studying them as I waited for my turn to face the panel of twenty.

After the panel interviews, the whole group reconvened in the conference room to await the announcement of the winner. I stared at the mahogany conference room table for what seemed like an eternity—until they awarded *me* the grant. Despite the good news, I couldn't pry my eyes from the tabletop when I realized that my biggest risk wasn't *losing* the grant, it was *winning* it. Now I had to deliver on the vision I had created, and I was scared of failing. There was nothing standing in the way of my achieving everything I had dreamed of—except me.

There are risks that hit you in the face and those you don't think about until after the fact. Inflation is one of those insidious risks that slink around in the shadows. Hidden from view until you least expect it, inflation can rob you of the earning power of your savings—if you let it. Inflation is the gradual erosion of the buying power of your money. Over the short term, inflation isn't that harmful. Where it gets you is in the long run. If you don't give your money a chance to grow, your money won't keep up with inflation and it will be worth less than when you first saved it.

Market Risk

Whenever you turn on the television or radio, read a newspaper or magazine, or talk to a money buddy, you probably hear about the stock market going up and down. Market risk is that volatility. The value of your investment may increase or decrease on a daily basis. Market risk is considered to be a short-term risk because over time it decreases as you look at the historical returns of investment types. However, market risk is substantial in the short term. Stock investments could lose a third or more of their value in the first year you purchase them, but if you hold your stocks for a ten-year period, your average earnings could be 9 percent.

Three Is a Magic Number

Do you remember the Schoolhouse Rock song "Three Is a Magic Number"? *A mother and father had a little baby. That makes three. Three is a magic number.*

Three is a magic number in investing as well. It's the number of basic investment types, called asset classes. *Stable values. Bonds. Stocks. That makes three, the magic number.*

What makes these three asset classes so magical is that it's the most important thing you need to know about investing. Gary Brinson, Randolph Hood, and Gilbert Beebower, famous economists who have spent their lives breaking new ground in finance, determined that 93.6 percent of the return on any investment has to do with asset allocation—what percentage is put in the basic investment types: stable values, bonds, and stocks. Less than 7 percent of the return has to do with investment selection (the stock or mutual fund) or timing the market (when you buy or sell the investment). Asset class is where it's at. And you only need to know those three.

Stocks are ownership shares in a company. You buy stock, you become an owner. You invest in stocks for long-term goals. Stocks are the most aggressive of the three asset classes, but they offer you the most opportunity for growth.

Bonds are an IOU to a government or corporation. You lend the money and are paid back principal and interest. Bonds are a more aggressive investment than stable values, but more conservative than stocks.

Stable values are investment contracts that keep your money safe. They include certificates of deposit (CDs) and money market accounts. Stable values, the least aggressive of the asset classes, are primarily a short-term investment because they are designed to protect your principal. On the flip side, they offer little opportunity for growth and generally don't keep pace with inflation over the long term.

It's All in the Mix

Ever made a Betty Crocker brownie mix? You combine the mix, an egg, and oil. Bake at 325 degrees and you have delicious goodies. Each ingredient on its own is not enough to make brownies. You get brownies when you put the ingredients all together and bake them. Change the mix or leave out the egg, and your brownies won't taste as good or may not turn out at all.

To spread your risk, you need to pay attention to the mix. You pick your mix based on your goal. If your goal is ten or more years away, your mix will include more stock, less bonds, and even less stable values. If your goal is less than three years away, your mix will include more stable values and little or no stocks and bonds.

Your personal mix will depend on your investment goal— when you need the money and what you'll use it for. The mix is usually based on your time frame and is adjusted by your risk tolerance. There is an abundance of tools and resources to help you select an investment mix. Here are a couple of places to check to get you started.

- **Your employer.** If you work for a large employer, chances are you have access to financial resources for retirement planning. Check out the information about your 401(k) plan. Use that plan to the IRS limits. Use the financial education resources your company provides to help you save and invest for retirement. Take advantage of any automated features, such as contribution escalation to increase your savings and automatic rebalancing to periodically align your portfolio back to your retirement strategy. Take advantage of premixed portfolios or targeted maturity lifecycle funds—professionally selected and managed investment mixes that are turnkey retirement strategies. All you need to do is pick one and invest all your retirement savings in it. You don't have to worry about the ongoing management of your portfolio—the experts do that for you.

- **CNNMoney.com asset allocation wizard.** Want a quick way to get an investment mix? Check out the asset allocation wizard on www.cnnmoney.com. Answer a few questions about your time frame and risk tolerance and you'll get an asset allocation that you can use as a model for your goal.

- **Vanguard.** Any mutual fund Web site will give you access to financial education and modeling tools to help you invest. But one way to implement your strategy is to invest in low-fee index funds. According to The Motley Fool, an investor Web site, more than 90 percent of mutual funds fail to outperform the indexes. That's because of the fees they charge and the fact that it's next to impossible to predict the performance of individual stocks. If you invest in index funds, you don't have the same fees associated with actively managed funds and you get the same performance as the indexes—so you get a better return. Vanguard has the reputation of offering index funds with low fees. Check out www.vanguard.com for more information.

I would like to end this section with a short reading list that will help you gain further insights into the investment strategies discussed here. These are all books that I have found extremely helpful in the investment workshops I teach to women:

- *The Average Family's Guide to Financial Freedom: How You Can Save a Small Fortune on a Modest Income* by Bill and Mary Toohey. This is a delightful book about how a family with a severely handicapped son lived a fun life, planned for retirement, parented their children, and left a legacy on a small income. This book describes in simple terms how to develop a money-saving mindset—how to spend less, invest wisely, and get more out of life.
- *Your Money Counts: The Biblical Guide to Earning, Spending, Saving, Investing, Giving and Getting Out of Debt* by Howard Dayton. Want to know what God says about money? Read this book. Dayton is CEO of Crown Financial Ministries and has extensive experience helping people bridge the spiritual-financial gap. The book explores the 2,350 Bible verses that provide everything you need to know about investing your money.
- *Money: A User's Manual: Avoiding Common Traps* by Bob Russell. This book gives clear scriptural guidance on how to use your possessions in a way that makes a clear difference for eternity. Russell helps you tackle investing from an ethical perspective and shows you how to avoid common investment traps.

4. SHARE WITH OTHERS

"To receive everything, one must first open one's hands and give."
—Taisen Deshimaru

From the time my son Liam could walk, he enjoyed sharing. Food, toys, bugs, dirt, drooly kisses, hugs. When he turned two, Liam started being a little more selective about what he gave away. But I still see the delight in his eyes when he presents his sister Gracie with a toy or when he breaks off half a cookie for a friend.

We start life as good sharers. We have to be. It's part of survival. The bond we formed with our mother or caretaker was built on the sharing of affection. At first, that's all we have to give—love. It remains the most important gift. Mother Teresa once said, "It is not how much we do, but how much love we put in the doing. It's not how we give, but how much love we put into the giving."

God wants you to give. And God wants you to be a cheerful giver. Sometimes that's difficult to do. If you're having trouble making ends meet, what do you have left to give? If you're making your bills but need to save for a home, retirement, or college for the kids—not to mention an emergency fund in case you get laid off—how do you prioritize giving? And how much should you give? And what good will come from giving?

Some people might argue that "giving" does not have to be just monetary—that you can give a portion of your time for service in a soup kitchen or at a local charity, or a portion of your mental energy and creativity in chairing committees at your church, or fundraising for the local battered women's shelter. However, while these kinds of activities are certainly worthy and admirable, there is a unique spiritual, psychological, and emotional energy that comes with giving actual money to your church or to whatever is your source of spiritual inspiration. Creating large amounts of energy does not necessarily mean giving immense amounts of dollars. It's the thought and the heart that count. Often, when you step out in faith and give, a deep psychological and spiritual "magic" blesses your effort and manifests in your life.

Trust and Tithing

I've experienced all of these struggles in my own life. The biggest decision for me was deciding whether or not to tithe at my church. Before I became a church member, tithing had not been in my vocabulary. It seemed like a foreign concept—giving 10 percent of your income away. What would happen to it? Wouldn't it be smarter to use it to set up my family? Why 10 percent? Is that net or gross? My mind kept struggling with the question of why do it and what I would get from it.

I asked my cousin Kourtney to share her ideas on tithing. She grew up in a Baptist church. Her parents regularly tithed, despite having six children and the care of our invalid grandmother. In fact, most members of that congregation tithed, despite having financial setbacks and numerous expenses and living on much less than a rock star's salary. When I asked Kourtney why she tithed, she simply said it's the right thing to do. It's God's money anyway and he pays you back with interest.

Proverbs 3:9 says "Honor the Lord with your wealth, with the firstfruits of all your crops." It's up to you to decide what "firstfruits" means in your family. Ten percent is the figure most often cited as the amount to be tithed to your church. Most spiritual guidance given on finances suggests tithing 10 percent, saving 10 percent, and living on 80 percent of what you make. However, the exact amount you give depends on your heart. God doesn't want your money if you give it begrudgingly.

In addition to tithing, Kourtney felt called to support a child in Africa. The monthly amount stretched her comfort level in making her monthly bills by $50. She prayed about it. The same month she started supporting the child, her salary increased and her taxes decreased, which exactly covered the $50 difference.

I thought that was a nice coincidence, but I was still skeptical. Down deep, I felt that tithing was the right thing to do, despite not being able to logically justify it with a return on my investment. So I stuck my toe in the water by tithing 10 percent of my bonus. The next day, my husband Denis was offered a great job at a great company, which more than made up for the amount tithed. The same fortunate coincidences continued when I began tithing my salary. My fear of not having enough didn't materialize. We made our bills, our children didn't go hungry, we continued to save for retirement and college educations, and we had enough for emergencies. The funny thing is, we still have money left over for other opportunities to give, such as to the victims of Hurricane Katrina and the tsunami in Thailand.

How does this happen? Isn't this just magical thinking? Doesn't this encourage reckless financial behavior—giving beyond your means and expecting God or others to clean up the mess if you go broke?

I don't believe so.

If you are practicing the other financial habits—spending less than you earn, systematically saving, and spreading your risk—you should have enough to give.

You get out of this life what you have the courage to give. If you love, you attract love to you. If you are respectful of the resources that God has given you and use them to make the world a better place, the world becomes a better place for you. Giving changes you and it changes the world you live in. By giving, you become stronger. You move out of the shadow of fear, empowered by your own action. By giving, you become more open to receiving back what you are giving. That's part of the magic. And by giving, your feelings of affection grow for the recipient of the gift. Love money grows with compound interest.

I thought Stephen Covey's *7 Habits of Highly Successful People* was just another book on business until my husband read me a passage where Covey counsels a man who has fallen out of love with his wife. "My friend, love is a verb. Love—the feeling—is the fruit of love, the verb. So love her. Serve her. Empathize. Appreciate. Affirm her. Are you willing to do that?"

If you give, you will get much more than you ever dreamed of.

You Get What You Give

Giving is power. Even if you don't feel like doing it, the very act opens your heart, allowing you to be affirmed and to receive a transfusion of positive energy. Giving benefits the giver just as much, or more so, than the recipient.

In *Nine Steps to Financial Freedom*, Suze Orman recounts how giving put her in a positive frame of mind when she was working for a brokerage firm. When you're feeling negative, people can sense it; they can smell it on you, even if you're talking to them on the phone. And they are repelled by it. Suze said she was having a low-energy day, decided to call in sick, and while she watched public television, a telethon came on. She made a donation and immediately began to feel better. That act of giving made her feel powerful and positive. She credits the giving to triggering an increase in new business that made her boatloads of money.

The act of giving changes the balance of power—in you and in the world. Positive energy replaces the negative as you share your time, your love, your resources. Like a magnet, you attract the very things you give away. Giving fills you with the power to create a new you. If you want to be more loving, love more. If you are praying for patience, practice being patient. If you want money, give it away.

Chapter Four

Practice Contentment

May 14, 1991, Bombay International Airport

It was 3 a.m., 103 degrees, and Bombay International Airport resembled Dante's Inferno. Hundreds of people were rushing in every direction, screaming in different dialects, and fighting to reach their destinations. My destination—the downtown Bombay YWCA—wouldn't be open for at least five hours. But standing outside the "Y" had to be better than hanging out in the airport. A kindly woman in a bright sari directed me to the bus downtown. I sat near the front, trying to determine what was dotting the roadside and median. It resembled strategically placed piles of garbage or the remnants of road construction. I started counting the piles and quickly lost track. Leaning over, I tapped the bus driver's shoulder and asked, "What's on the side of the road?"

"People," he said.

In Detroit, it's pretty common to see the homeless wandering the streets—maybe ten or twenty, but not hundreds or thousands in one place. The vast extent of homelessness in India was overwhelming. How did all these people end up like this? Imagine driving down I-75 on your way to Comerica Park for a Tiger's game and all you see on the roadside from the Ambassador Bridge to Woodward Avenue (more than ten miles) is homeless people in sleeping bags. I was experiencing my own version of Deli belly—nausea from seeing true poverty. And no amount of medication could wipe the image from my mind.

The driver continued, "In the wintertime, a truck comes around to pick up the dead." His words changed my perception of money and possessions forever. From that moment on, I could no longer take for granted the comfort of my home, the value of my education, and my infinite worth as a human being. As I made my way through the rest of the thirteen countries on my itinerary, I noticed that when I tried to ignore poverty, it loomed larger. When I turned a kind eye to those in need and provided support, I felt connected to a purpose greater than myself and I felt a profound sense of peace from knowing I was working in a small way toward a solution. Instead of feeling powerless in the face of despair, I saw possibility. This led to a long journey of reevaluating my own limiting beliefs about wealth, what I'm on earth to do, and how my resources are a gift to trigger positive change.

The Power of Comparison

Half the world lives on less than $2.50 a day. If you're privileged enough to be born in a part of the world where you're living on more—congratulations! The question is, How do you feel about what you have? Do you feel rich?

I don't know you. I don't know how much you have in your bank account. I don't know what your job or family situation is. But I know one thing about you—God has blessed you and you are truly rich. It's up to you to realize that truth and appreciate what you have.

No matter how much time has passed, I can still see the faces of the street children I met in Bombay. Their hungry, naked, dirty bodies and their haunting eyes touched the core of my soul and left me with a conviction about the immense value of each life. These children had no possessions. They had no parents, home, or financial security. Still they lived each moment fully and celebrated life—far more than I did with my infinitely greater financial resources and possessions. They had something to teach me—that I am much more than my material resources, that dwelling on how much money I had or how I could make more was making me miserable. Through them I realized that unless I started to live and use my resources for a greater good, I would miss my opportunity to experience the greatest wealth of all— giving and sharing from a full heart.

It's human nature to compare ourselves with others. We use our eyes and ears to gather information that reinforces what we already think about ourselves. If we feel great about our place in the world, we'll gather evidence that supports our inner harmony. We'll notice the beauty of where we live. We'll sense the love and innocence of others. We'll grant others the benefit of the doubt because we allow it for ourselves. We'll see opportunities for success and joy instead of obstacles.

However, if we feel insecure about our future, fearful of losing what we have, or unworthy of our birthright to live a joyful life, we'll find equally compelling evidence that reinforces our own internal hell. Life will seem like a struggle—endless days of toil and trouble. Ugliness will pervade what we see in our home, in our relationships, and in ourselves. Friends will seem in short supply. It will appear that God is gone or doesn't exist.

When you focus on what's missing, you will manifest more of that in your life. For example, Melissa often told her daughters "we can't afford it" when they asked her for toys or candy on the family's frequent shopping trips. One day, Melissa woke up and realized that saying those words over and over again had caused her to feel depressed. All of the things she wanted—family vacations, a larger home, recreation—appeared to be more and more out of reach. She realized that she had been sending a clear message to the universe: "No, I don't want your help." These powerful words closed down any possibility of receiving wealth. However, when Melissa became aware of her self-limiting beliefs after attending a transformational workshop, she began to see herself as the source of wealth. She began to use her words to create the wealth she desired by saying things such as "I am open to the possibility of moving into a beautiful home that's right for my family." Within three months, she and her family moved into a home similar to the one she had pictured in her mind.

I live in Orange County, California, and I am a living testament to the internal conflict created by comparison. If I don't make a daily conscious decision to focus on my blessings, I hear an ongoing internal dialogue between my better self and the self that thinks I should be doing better. It kind of goes like this:

Do I have the right car, clothes, hairstyle, handbag, and diaper bag? *You shop at Target and don't wear makeup.*

Am I thin enough, smart enough, cultured enough, well-traveled enough, popular enough? *You spend so much time at home with the kids—why don't you get out and get a life.*

Do my children have the right clothes, toys, books, and videos? *You got those at a secondhand store.*

Do my children go to the right schools, have the right friends, and eat the right things? *Hot dogs and fish sticks. Don't your children deserve better?*

The power of comparison is like a magnifying glass—it helps you zero in on whatever you put under it. *What* you choose to magnify is powerfully influenced by what you allow yourself to think and dream, what you watch on television, what you read, who you talk to, the friends you spend time with, where and how often you shop, and what you do. Some of this you can't control, such as when you're surfing the Internet and a pop-up ad catches you by surprise, or a deluge of credit card applications arrive in the mail, or a telemarketer calls you during dinnertime. But most of the time, you *can* choose what you put in your head.

Where contentment is concerned, your mental diet is as important as your physical one. Feed a brain a steady diet of *Cosmopolitan* and *Vogue* and inevitably that brain will think that the average size for a woman is two and that it's a biological right to own a Prada bag and matching shoes. That brain will think those airbrushed models are real and condemn the body it is housed in for not looking like the images it sees.

The Keys to Contentment

Contentment is not some mystical feeling conjured up by being in the right place at the right time with the right people. It doesn't come from having the right things. Contentment is the realization that at any given moment, God has given you everything you need to have a joyful life.

Like a muscle, the power of contentment can be strengthened by what you believe in and what you focus on. To build your contentment:

- Believe in abundance
- Catalog your blessings
- Limit your exposure
- Enrich your world

Believe in Abundance

Humans are born into a conversation of scarcity around money, love, and time. No matter what culture we live in, we buy into the belief that these resources are in short supply. This belief is simply wrong.

According to Lynne Sheridan, a WorldWorks trainer and a doctoral student, if you took all the money in the world and divided it equally among the planet's inhabitants, everyone would have more than $1.2 million, so there's no lack of money in the world.

Money flows to those who are open to receiving it. And as you give money freely, you get it freely. Just like love. Love grows as you give love. The same thing with time—it is not an objective reality, but a human-created measuring system. Reminding us that time is actually more plentiful and flexible than we are prepared to acknowledge, Lynne says, "We aren't short of time. Time is all we have." We are all infinite beings— we can choose to be abundant in time, money, and love. The key is reframing the conversation of scarcity and limitation to a conversation that empowers you. A mother who says she doesn't have time for anything will indeed find herself hurried, frazzled, and burned out. A mother who says she has all the time in the world for her children will find herself creating meaningful, powerful, and connected moments with her children, which produce a lifetime of memories. There is no scarcity of anything in the universe. Use language to create the abundant, beautiful life you imagine.

Take the concept of abundant love. When I became pregnant with my daughter, Grace, I foolishly believed that there was no way I could love another baby the way that I loved my son, Liam. At the time, he had just turned two. How would he act when I brought a new baby home? Would he think I was being disloyal to him by taking care of her? But Grace found her way into all our hearts. Adding another child to the equation didn't deplete the supply of love, but multiplied it. I found I had more love not only for *my* children, but also for children outside the family. I found myself filled with more kindness, compassion, and love not only for the people I knew, but also for those I didn't know. Liam quickly grew fond of Gracie, and I noticed his relationships with other preschoolers benefited as well. He was quicker to show love and to share with others.

If you train yourself to think abundantly, then you can rejoice in another's success and not be threatened by it. There is no need to be jealous when you see good things happen to others, because you know that you are already blessed and that more blessings are coming your way. By wishing people success and rejoicing in their success, you attract success to yourself. You get what you give. Your thoughts shape your actions. Your actions yield results.

Believing in abundance takes practice. Fear is ever-present in our minds and it's fear that leads to scarcity thinking. Somehow we think the success of others will overshadow us and that there will be nothing left for us—that we will be on the outside looking in, alone, unloved, unworthy. It takes practice to suspend our belief in a reality painted by fear. When you find yourself slipping into scarcity thinking, identify the trigger of this feeling and recognize that what you are feeling is not reality. Remind yourself of the abundance of love and wealth that is available to you and say a prayer to restore your perspective.

When I attended Michigan State University, I applied for just about every scholarship and grant available to help pay for tuition, including a golf writing scholarship. I had never been to a golf course and had never watched golf on television, but I decided to apply for the scholarship because it paid the most: $4,000 over four years. Although I made the finalist round, the scholarship went to Gail, a beautiful blonde debutante from an affluent Oakland County suburb. My jealousy blinded me to the fact that she got the scholarship because she deserved it— she actually knew about golf and could write about it. We were both staff writers for *The State News* and I could barely bring myself to look at her, let alone congratulate her. I kept thinking to myself, "She already has money. Why did that scholarship go to her?" Envy rotted inside of me until I'd finally had enough. I congratulated her on winning the scholarship and I started praying for her success. At first it felt a little silly—she was already successful, so why should I pray for her? But as I began praying for her, positive things started happening for me. I got a summer internship at *The News-Herald*, a Downriver Detroit newspaper, and won a couple of awards from the Detroit Press Club. The combination helped cover a good chunk of my college costs.

If ever you feel weak or worried, if ever you feel scarcity thinking coming on strong, if ever you feel that success is beyond your grasp, if ever you feel someone is standing in your way— pray. Pray away all your fears. Sincerely pray for enlightenment—to see things as they actually are, not how we've twisted them to be.

Ask for a miracle. According to Marianne Williamson, a miracle is simply a change in perception, and it's her belief that we don't ask for enough miracles from God. Ask God to guide your thoughts and actions. Ask God to bless the person who is causing you trouble. Look inside yourself; don't blame circumstances or others. Focusing on things beyond your control won't lead to peace or contentment. Conserve your energy, save your emotions, direct your focus to what you *can* do to improve your life. A slight change in perception can have miraculous results. All you have to do is ask for it.

Catalog Your Blessings

You are a child of God. You have a rich heritage. You are truly blessed. Once you believe this and live this, contentment will become a part of your DNA. If you catalog your blessings, you'll see *all* that God has given you.

But don't stop at the things you consider a blessing. Every aspect of your life can be looked upon as a blessing. God's wisdom leads us to situations that help us grow. Often we don't immediately see them as blessings. What turns our everyday encounters into blessed events is how we choose to see them. Consider this prayer, written by an unknown Confederate soldier during the Civil War:

> *I asked God for strength, that I might achieve —*
> *I was made weak, that I might learn humbly to obey.*
> *I asked for health, that I might do greater things —*
> *I was given infirmity, that I might do better things.*
> *I asked for riches, that I might be happy —*
> *I was given poverty, that I might be wise.*
> *I asked for power, that I might have the praise of men —*
> *I was given weakness, that I might feel the need of God.*
> *I asked for all things, that I might enjoy life —*
> *I was given life that I might enjoy all things.*
> *I got nothing that I asked for —*

But everything that I had hoped for.
Despite myself, all my prayers were answered.
I am, among all persons, most richly blessed.

God has richly blessed your life. Stop. Take stock of what God has given you. In fact, write down what you have, reflect on the list, and give thanks.

The Biggest Blessing: People

Start by listing all the people in your life: those you love, those you like, those you dislike, those you're indifferent to. God put those people in your life for a reason. There is something you can learn from every one of them. Bless and truly appreciate all the people in your life. Pray for them regularly—especially those you find unlovable. Spend time with them and cherish those relationships, because this will strengthen the friendships as well as benefit you.

"Recent research suggests that regularly seeing good friends in the local park will bring a greater boost to mental health than having a shiny German automobile parked outside your home," said Professor Andrew Oswald, professor of economics at England's University of Warwick. "My candid advice to aging Americans would be to use your hard-earned cash to invest much more in friendships than in material items."

This is not to say, however, that we should let just anyone and anything into our lives. It is important to be discriminating about the people we drop our guard around and with whom we spend our time. There's a big difference between grouchy but harmless Aunt Tilly and people who are truly toxic, emotional vampires who will drain you if you let them. There are some relationships you should *not* cherish and people you should *not* spend time around because they will harm you emotionally and spiritually. Trust your feelings and use your God-given judgment.

Second Biggest Blessing: Health

If you have your health, you are truly blessed. As I get so caught up in rushing to the next big thing, I often forget the miraculous nature of the body I've been given. The key to appreciating your health is taking a moment to marvel at what you've been given.

At seven months old, my daughter Grace was fascinated by her hands. She spent the good part of a day rotating her wrists to examine the front and back of each hand. She'd stop in the middle of eating or playing with a toy to look at her appendages. "Wow, these are mine!" she seemed to gurgle.

We need to celebrate and cherish our health. It will not only make us more content, but in the long run will also save us a boatload of money on medical expenses. In today's environment of 10 to 12 percent annual increases in health care costs, improving your health today and maintaining good health into the future can make the difference between a comfortable retirement and just scraping by.

Take stock of your health. What sort of shape are you in? Get a physical and find out—it may be free through your health care insurance. Do you have a chronic condition that needs to be addressed, such as diabetes or asthma? If so, find out if your company offers a disease management program and use it. How do you feel? Does your body ache? Are you weighed down with stress and excess weight? Go take a walk, ride a bike, or do yoga.

Now is the time to appreciate your current level of health and invest in improving it. No matter what condition you are in physically, it's never too late to thank God for what you have been given and to make changes to live a more healthful lifestyle. Your body is the vessel that God gave you to enjoy life. It's up to you to properly nourish it physically, mentally, spiritually, and emotionally so that you can live your best life.

Other Blessings

If you have friends and health, you're truly wealthy. But there are other things God has blessed you with. Write those down as well. If you have a house, appreciate it by taking care of it. If you feel restless and think that you need a bigger house, clean the one you have. The more you care for something, the more you will appreciate it. The same goes for a car. If you feel like you need a brighter, shinier, newer car, start taking better care of the one you have. If you feel you have nothing to wear, thank God that you have the clothes you have. Before you eat a meal, say a blessing and give thanks that you have something to eat.

My mother spent her childhood in fear of not having enough food. Her father, an orphan by age four, cleaned out bars before school, ate what others threw away, and spent his adult life searching for a secure job. There were many nights she went to bed hungry, wondering where her next meal would come from. To this day, she has a tremendous appreciation of food and shows her love by feeding others. When someone cooks something for her, she claps for the chef. When I find myself lapsing into apathy over cooking dinner or eating a meal, I think about what it must have been like for her. I thank God for what I have and I feel deeply satisfied.

Limit Your Exposure

According to a South Dakota Department of Health study, the average American male spends twenty-nine hours watching TV each week; the average female spends thirty-four hours. As I mentioned earlier, each hour of television you watch may increase your annual spending by as much as $208. One of the contributing factors to "competitive spending" among Americans is a shift in whom we compare ourselves with. It used to be that people compared themselves with their neighbors. Now we compare ourselves with coworkers, who may make three to five times more than our neighbors do. Or we compare ourselves with what we see on TV, which usually portrays "middle-class Americans" living lifestyles that only the superrich could afford. TV programs have skewed our sense of reality, brainwashing us to believe that we *deserve* what others have.

To live a contented life, you need to limit your exposure to negative influences. Start by turning off the television. In fact, if you can stomach it, get rid of your television sets altogether. The same with magazines. An hour-long television show has roughly twenty minutes of content and forty minutes of commercials—traditional commercial breaks as well as product placement in the show itself. Each magazine you buy is more than 75 percent packed with advertisements. Take a *Cosmopolitan* or *GQ* and cut out all the ads. What do you have left? Does the magazine look like Swiss cheese? You're digesting those images every time you turn on the television or open a magazine. Those images color your thoughts, expectations, and level of contentment.

Even if you intellectually know that you don't need what's being sold, marketers catch your attention and the seed is planted in your mind. It may not take root immediately, but cumulatively the constant attack of advertisers will wear down your armor.

Consider when General Motors built one of its first plants in rural Mexico. After workers received a couple of paychecks, they stopped coming back. They had what they needed to provide for their families. What got them to come back to work? Catalogs. When the workers started receiving catalogs, suddenly their wants became needs and they were back to work, fueled by the desires stoked by marketers.

Limiting your exposure to negative influences includes negative people. If there is someone in your life who makes you feel anxious or competitive or who causes you to feel insecure or self-conscious, take a step back and hold awareness for what you are feeling. Ask yourself why you are feeling this way. Test to see if your behavior changes as the result of being in contact with this person. Don't get me wrong; you can't shut yourself off from reality. You will need to continue working or interacting with some unpleasant people, regardless of how they make you feel. But realize that God put that person in your life to teach you something. Ask what it is you're supposed to learn. Learn it and move on.

Enrich Your World

The most powerful antidote to discontentment is finding your purpose in life. What has God put you on this earth to do? For each of us, that purpose is different. We were each uniquely crafted to make a personal contribution. If you are living for yourself, you're missing the point.

"Busyness is a great enemy of relationships," says Rick Warren, author of *The Purpose Driven Life—What On Earth Am I Here For?* "We become preoccupied with making a living, doing our work, paying bills, and accomplishing goals as if these are the point of life. They are not. The point of life is learning to love—God and people. Life minus love equals zero."

To receive love, we need to give love. To enrich our lives, we need to give of ourselves. To be content, we need to throw ourselves into purposeful work that makes this world a better place. Most people are more concerned about what their neighbor drives than how many children are dying of starvation. It's easy to live our insulated lives and think that everyone else is just like us—that they want the same things, have access to food, education, and opportunity, and can change their lives in an instant.

In order to understand how most of the world lives, you need to experience it for yourself. No amount of watching PBS or the Discovery channel can stand in for traveling to the source, touching the people, doing the work, seeing the effect. Sending money is great. But if your goal is true contentment, sign up for a trip to India or Africa or Asia.

If you are still unsure about your purpose in life, you can use the 21-day journal as a powerful tool to help you connect with your passions and your reason for being here—and to put that energy into motion in your daily life and in the greater world around you.

CHAPTER FIVE

PASS IT ON

"There are many wonderful things that will never be done if you do not do them."

—The Honorable Charles D. Gill

The time has come to put into practice what you've learned so far. You know that God loves you, that you are priceless, and that you have a unique purpose on this planet—that your self-worth is independent of your net worth. God has given you everything you need at this moment to live a rich life. Now that you have begun to develop new perspectives about how to use your financial and spiritual resources more wisely so that they will grow and flourish, it's time to begin thinking about passing this information along to someone who can benefit from it; perhaps someone younger than you for whom you can be a mentor. By doing so, you will not only reinforce your own learning, but you also may improve the life of another.

Every thought you think, every dime you spend, every word you say has a ripple effect throughout the world. You can actively choose to create positive energy that will affect those around you. Some of those you touch will pass it on themselves, becoming more cheerful and charitable to those they encounter just because you chose to say something nice to them.

Once when I was in Moscow, a scowling desk clerk met my gaze as I crossed the lobby of the government hotel where I was assigned to stay. She controlled whether or not I could exchange U.S. dollars for local currency so that I could buy breakfast. It was in my best interest to become her friend. But how? A squarish elderly woman, she looked like she hadn't cracked a smile since Stalin was alive. I pulled out a couple pieces of Juicy Fruit gum and placed them on the counter in front of her as a peace offering. Then I made my request. I'm not sure if she even heard me. As she gazed at the gum, her face became luminous. Her hostility melted away. She simply said, "For my grandchildren." No other words were needed.

I didn't see the desk clerk again after I gave her the gum, but I can imagine the ripple effect that God created: She took the bus home, probably retaining the same luminous quality on her face in anticipation of presenting her grandchildren with the gift. Others picked up on the positive energy she radiated— this feeling of well-being was caught by some of her fellow passengers. She got off the bus, made her way to her daughter's home and found her grandchildren. Barely able to contain her love, she hugged her grandchildren and gave each a stick of gum. They laughed and showed the sticks to their mother before putting them in their mouths. Mother and father were happy because the children were happy. Maybe the next day the grandma recounted to coworkers the story of the unexpected present. It goes on and on.

Little things add up. Little by little as we change the way we look at the world and use our resources, we change it for the better. But these little actions can add up only if you actually take the time to do them. You can't delegate acts of kindness and love. Put off doing them and you lose your power. Apathy is more insidious than pesticide. Don't poison the world.

You spread poison each time you "sin." In *The Four Agreements*, Don Miguel Ruiz says that sin is anything you do against yourself. Since we are all connected, a sin against yourself ultimately affects others. If you say something mean about someone else, it boomerangs back at you because that person is likely to find out about it and hate you. You spread poison when you gossip, judge others, envy others, hoard, hate, spend recklessly, rack up debt, kill another's dream, steal, lie, murder, and are apathetic toward injustice.

Rosa Parks, a civil rights heroine, once took a stand against segregation by sitting in the white-only section of a bus. Reflecting on her act of defiance, Parks said, "I wasn't tired physically, or no more tired than I usually was at the end of a working day. No, the only tired I was, was tired of giving in."

On the passing of Rosa Parks in 2005, an eloquent Alabama state representative recounted the impact of her role in repealing the Jim Crow laws, and talked about the others who had gone before her, paving the way with nonviolent acts of protest. When a journalist asked why the other acts hadn't received as much attention as Rosa Parks sitting in the front of the bus, the representative attributed it to her character. He said that Rosa Parks was known as a good woman, an active member of her church, a thoughtful and gentle citizen. As she was taken into police custody, word spread: "Did you hear what happened to Rosa Parks?" Everyone knew she was not a criminal and that her act was in defiance of an unjust system.

Your actions matter deeply to God. Hold awareness for what you are doing. Handle your words and resources wisely. Ask for guidance in your daily actions.

Teach Your Children

"We will not hide these truths from our children but will tell the next generation about the glorious deeds of the Lord. We will tell of his power and the mighty miracles he did...so the next generation might know them—even the children not yet born—that they in turn might teach their children. So each generation can set its hope anew on God, remembering his glorious miracles and obeying his commands." Psalm 78:4, 6–7 (NLT)

You have the opportunity to enrich the lives of the next generation by role modeling good financial behaviors and by helping others learn how to handle money. Although I use the frame of the parent-child relationship, you don't need to be a parent to pass on what you've learned. In fact, if you know *anyone* younger than you, you have the opportunity to help them learn good financial habits. This section applies to everyone who has the heart to help others. Even if you don't, do it anyway, because you will benefit from it.

According to a 2005 Dartmouth-Hitchcock medical study, children begin modeling the behavior of adults as early as age two. I can tell you from experience that they start earlier than that. From nine months old onward, my daughter Gracie has tried to brush her teeth and walk up and down stairs as she sees me do. When I brush my teeth, she squeals and grasps for a toothbrush. She wants to be a big girl, and her current level of proficiency doesn't stop her from trying.

In most families, money is a taboo subject and is generally avoided. Ironically, according to Jessie O'Neill, author of *The Golden Ghetto: The Psychology of Affluence*, this is especially true in wealthy families. Financial behaviors and lessons are "caught," not taught.

Your children hear every word you use, watch every move you make, and watch every dollar you spend or save. They will draw their own conclusions unless you provide the right context and reinforce the message. That puts parents in a quandary. According to Joline Godfrey, author of *Raising Financially Fit Kids*, "…although 75 percent of parents think that providing financial guidance for their kids is a moral imperative, only 36 percent report having any clarity on how to do it."

Though never overtly discussed, money messages modeled by our parents and/or caretakers shaped our hopes, dreams, and fears as youngsters and still shadow us today. If you lived in fear of not having enough, to some extent that insecurity lingers in you today. If you never had to worry about money or never had to deal with it, to some extent that security fortifies you today. Those feelings may have nothing to do with reality. You may be financially independent for life and still be haunted by the threat of poverty. Or, your finances may be a wreck, yet you are living as if someone else will take care of the mess.

Those underlying feelings about money will seep and creep into what you teach your children, so be honest with yourself about what you believe. List what you think and feel about money. Bring those beliefs out in the light. Recognize them. Face them. Compare them against reality. Is there a disconnect? Realize that you control what you think about and do with your money. You can reprogram yourself with more positive attitudes about using your resources and, in turn, pass those beliefs on to your children.

Start Early

From birth, you knew your mother's (or caretaker's) voice. You could read her like a book. Like infant telepathy, you learned her moods, fears, loves, and lessons. She passed them on to you.

In the same way, you affect the children whose lives you touch. Whether it be your son or daughter, your niece or nephew, your grandchild, a student, a neighbor's child, or a friend's child, realize that children pick up money messages early.

According to S. I. Hayakawa, author of *Language in Thought and Action,* "Very small infants understand the love, warmth, or the irritation in a mother's voice long before they are able to understand her words. Most children retain this sensitivity to pre-symbolic elements in language. It even survives in some adults; they are the people credited with 'intuition' or 'unusual tact.' Their talent lies in their ability to interpret tones of voice, facial expressions, and other symptoms of the internal condition of the speaker: they listen not only to *what* is said, but *how* it is said."

Money messages come through loud and clear. In fact, they are amplified in our culture because money means so many different things to different people. Talk openly with your children about money. Remove the taboo. Teach them that money is, above all, a resource for putting their values into action. Teach them to love God, love others, and live a life respectful of what they are given.

Start sending these positive messages early. Waiting until they are able to talk about money is too late. This doesn't mean force-feeding your fourteen-month-old the *Wall Street Journal.* It does mean talking to your infant in a way that affirms his or her self-worth, connection to God, and responsibility to make the world a better place.

When your child is old enough to know what money is, clarify the definition. Position money as a resource to do good in the world, not as a tool of self-gratification and overindulgence or a measure of self-worth. Making money isn't a contest to be won or a commodity to be collected and hoarded.

Teach your child how to handle money by giving her an allowance. Divide the allowance into three categories: save, spend, and give. Help her think about her wants and needs and how to balance those competing interests. Help her decide how much to save for her future, while satisfying some of her wants and needs and giving to a church, charity, or good cause. Start early to encourage socially responsible thinking. If you would like her to tithe, explain why and help her practice it until she can make a choice about whether she wants to continue doing so.

When Liam was two and a half, he discovered money. Finding some of his uncle's pocket change on the floor, Liam picked it up and ran around the house shouting, "Money, money, money!" I began giving him a weekly allowance equaling his age—two dollars in quarters. In addition, Denis and I presented him with three plastic containers labeled "Save," "Spend," and "Give." That Sunday in church and ever since, I have helped him put part of the allowance in the offering and reaffirm his choice to give. I'm sure he doesn't grasp the full extent of what he is doing, but that's okay. Eventually he will. In the meantime, it gives me an opportunity to clarify *my* values and pass them along to him. When he is ready to make his own choices, he will be ready.

Be a Role Model

"Talking, walking, and eating are the same: we start early and by watching others, making mistakes, and trying again and again, over time we get more skilled and sophisticated," states Joline Godfrey in *Raising Financially Fit Kids*. The same goes for handling money.

Be careful what you do. Little eyes are watching you. Little ears are listening to you. I learned this the hard way one afternoon when I took both kids with me to the 4:30 p.m.

95

Saturday service at Saddleback Church. The church campus is huge, especially when you are schlepping a toddler and an infant. When we were making the pilgrimage back to the car, I noticed that the snaps holding the legs of Liam's overalls together had come totally unfastened, making his overalls look like a long skirt flapping in the gusty wind. Since I was holding Gracie on my right hip and we were half a mile away from the car, this wasn't a safe spot to park Gracie to refasten Liam's pants. My solution was to walk faster. However, Liam decided at that moment that it would be a good idea to remove his diaper, and he managed to get it almost completely off. Hoisting him to my left hip, I walked even faster. When Liam decided to pee, I knew it was all over. If not for the wind, we might have been able to make it to the car without causing a scene, but it was obvious what had happened. The kind crossing guard who stopped traffic so I could cross to the parking lot said, "Boy, you have your hands full." We finally arrived at the car. I parked Liam in the front passenger seat while I buckled Gracie, who was screaming by then, into her car seat. At the moment that I reached over to grab hold of Liam and put him into his seat, he latched onto the rearview mirror and pulled it off. The words "your father is going to kill you" slipped out of my mouth before I could stop them. Another wailing child to buckle into the car seat.

When we got home, my brother-in-law was in the driveway, so I asked him if he could fix the mirror—hoping to keep the fiasco from my husband. And we almost got away with it except for one thing: The next day, Liam remembered what I'd said to him and recited his new vocabulary lesson: "Daddy, I'm going to kill you."

Just as our words and deeds model behavior to our children, so do our attitudes and actions around money. Be careful what you think, say, and do about finances in the presence of your children. If you want your children to be financial geniuses, you need to first be one yourself.

So, be the behavior you want to see in their lives. If you tell your child to tithe and then you close your purse when the offering plate comes along, there's a disconnect. If you tell your child to limit her spending, but your credit cards are all maxed out, there's a disconnect. If you tell your child to save for her future, but you don't save for your retirement, there's a disconnect. If you tell your child to diversify, but you're invested only in company stock or you don't invest at all, there's a disconnect. You will create confusion and lose the credibility to influence your child.

The key to raising a financially responsible adult is to be one yourself. If you want your child to live within her means, create a budget for yourself first. Share it with her. Show her the household income and expenses. Help her get her arms around cash flow—how much is coming into the house and how much is going out. Show her how much is set aside for saving and giving. Show her your 401(k) statement. Show her how much you are saving for her college and how much it will cost.

Shop and Invest Responsibly

Remember the television ad "Look for the union label"? It encouraged shoppers to stop and flip the label to see if what they were buying was made by U.S. union workers. Today, we live in a much smaller world where the lines are blurred between where a company is headquartered and where products are produced. Increasingly, there's no correlation. A car could be designed in Detroit, assembled in Mexico, and sold in Singapore.

Your value system is reflected not only by what you buy, but also by what company you buy it from, what their value system is, what their suppliers' and partners' value systems are, how their workers are treated, whether or not they exploit labor in developing countries, and how all responsible parties treat the environment. In essence, you need to look at the label and do some investigating.

As you teach your children about smart investment, don't forget the lessons in *ethical* investment. For example, in Tom and David Gardner's book *The Motley Fool Investment Guide for Teens: 8 Steps to Having More Money Than Your Parents Ever Dreamed Of*, they encourage teens to buy the stock of companies that keep people coming back for more. Two of the examples they use are Philip Morris and Starbucks, because each offers addictive products. They acknowledge the inner conflict that might be created by investing in Philip Morris, since the company profits (at least in part) from cigarette sales. But the authors state their position that those who buy cigarettes are consenting adults and as long as the company is not doing anything illegal, they don't have a problem buying the stock. Plus, the company offers handsome dividends. They do have a point. I thought about buying Philip Morris for my kids, but I couldn't bring myself to do it—no matter what the current level of dividends. Bottom line is that I don't want my children, anyone else's children, or any person on the planet to smoke. It's not good for them. It's not good for the environment. And I've seen too many good people die of cancer.

Now, I didn't have the same problem with Starbucks. I drink their coffee too often myself to discount it as an investment.

When you shop or invest, ask questions. Encourage your children to do the same. Begin to research the companies you buy from. Know if the company is a good corporate citizen. Know if they care about the planet. If their moral compass doesn't have a pointer, direct your business elsewhere.

Use Resources

There are numerous books out there that can help teach your children the real deal about money. Here are some good ones:

Raising Financially Fit Kids **by Joline Godfrey** is an easy-to-read, practical guide that doesn't stop with saving and investing, but encourages entrepreneurialism, getting paid what you're worth, and learning how to use money to change the world. Packed with age-appropriate practices to coach your kids, Joline weaves in real-life stories from parents and children and the challenges they face. Her "life money map" helps you create a financial apprenticeship for your child starting as early as age five and continuing until age eighteen.

Growing Money: A Complete Investing Guide for Kids **by Gail Karlitz.** Full of fun examples, this book breaks down investing into simple, actionable steps. It even has an investor personality quiz for children age nine or older. Clear bar charts and graphs help bring financial concepts home.

Fun with Money **by Kathie Billingslea Smith.** This book is a great primer for teaching your kids how to shop wisely and resist the lures of consumerism. The book includes a stash of paper coins that can be used to purchase items on the pages. You're guided through an imaginary trip to a toy store, book store, and ice cream shop for a hands-on experience with money.

Moneymakers: Good Cents for Girls **by Ingrid Roper and Susan Synarski.** Want to encourage the entrepreneurial spirit in your daughter? This book helps kids stretch their imagination and learn the ropes of starting their own kiddy enterprise. Full of great ideas, it even has photos of young women who share their stories of success.

YOUR 21-DAY JOURNAL

DISCOVER YOUR BLESSED LIFE

Most financial goal setting falls apart because we come at it from the wrong place. We think things such as "If only I was rich, everything would be different. I wouldn't be afraid. I'd be happy. I'd be a better person." But wealth only exaggerates our shortcomings and creates new problems to replace the old ones. Think of all those lottery winners whose lives became a living hell after they won the jackpot. According to Kevin O'Keefe, author of *The Average American*, 75 percent of Americans who win the lottery lose all of their money within five years. The more you focus on wealth, the more illusive it will be. You may earn it, but if you don't learn how to invest and spend it intelligently, you'll lose it through mismanagement. Wealth becomes available and sustainable when you use it for God's purpose.

Discovering your blessed life is an inside-out process. Start with the soul. Most of us aren't in the habit of thinking about wealth this way, so we need to form a new habit. Behavioral experts say it takes approximately 21 days to form a habit. Use this journal to discover your blessed life. All you have to do each day is set aside thirty minutes of quiet time, sit down in your favorite spot, and from your heart, write about the three Ds: dream, define, and do. Dreaming will open up new possibilities. Defining will help focus your energy. Doing will help you cement your learning and give you a sense of accomplishment. Begin by asking for God's blessing, and then unleash your imagination.

A word of warning before you begin your journey: When you start living your life according to God's purpose, buckle up, because you're in for the ride of your life. The world will begin to move in ways you never anticipated. Opportunities will seem to magically appear. Your new awareness will bring them to your attention. It will be like *you've* won the lottery, but the payout will be different. Ironically, as you see your material wealth grow, the material part of your life will become less important to you. In fact, as your material wealth grows, it will pale in comparison to the bigger payoff—a greater connection to your Source Power.

I've seen the power of journaling materialize in my own life. As I started writing this book, John Henry McDonald urged me to start actively creating my life by writing about what I wanted in the spiritual, emotional, mental, physical, and fiscal realms. For 21 days, I followed the discipline and cut out pictures of what I wanted in my life. One thing that emerged as important was a more loving, connected relationship with my husband Denis. I cut out a picture of Denis and me when we first started dating—one that showed us holding hands and gazing deeply into each other's eyes. I detailed what I wanted to feel when I looked at him, the ways of being I wanted manifested in our relationship. By taking the time to truly become the architect of my marital relationship, my wish was granted. After eleven years of marriage, Denis and I are more connected and dedicated to one another than ever before.

I took a stand for what I wanted to create financially. I pasted pictures of culturally diverse women into the pages of my journal and wrote my personal mission statement to economically empower women worldwide. I wrote down the effects I wanted to have on their lives and how I wanted to use my resources to accomplish transformation. What resulted was this book, worldwide speaking engagements, connected relationships with other powerful people on a mission to transform the world, and unlimited support—financial, emotional, spiritual, mental, and physical—in accomplishing my mission.

Ready to claim your riches? Start writing. Only 5 percent of Americans write down their goals—and, coincidentally, that same 5 percent are the most affluent. Here are some suggestions to guide your journey:

1. Enter this daily appointment on your calendar. Reserve thirty minutes of quiet time each day. Know that the payoff is worth it—the next 21 days will transform your life.

2. Pray for God's guidance. With every step, every thought, every wish, every intention, ask for God to be there for you. Whenever you become discouraged, restate your intention. Remember, you *have* not because you *ask* not. Ask!

3. Act in faith first. From this point forward, you are not allowed to worry. God will reward you, but you need to demonstrate your faith before you see a financial result. Thoughts have energy. Actions are powerful. If, on a daily basis, your intent is to change the world in some positive way, you will uncover resources and strength you never thought possible.

DAY 1

CHOOSE TO LIVE IN A
FRIENDLY UNIVERSE

Einstein said the most important decision in your life is to decide, Do I live in a friendly universe or a hostile universe? That one decision affects your entire existence. From that answer springs infinite possibilities or endless obstacles.

We think in frames. Frames are the mental shortcuts we use to put our existence in perspective. They shape how we view things. Once we set up a frame, we hardly ever revisit it—we accept it as truth. And if something doesn't match up with our frame—some bit of new information, a thought, data, etc.—we immediately reject it. It's kind of like going through life wearing blinders. We can't see new possibilities for thought and action because we are stuck in old patterns that no longer serve us.

Therefore, how you view the universe affects your ability to dream, plan, ask for help, or do anything. If you think the universe is against you, your mind will constantly look for evidence to support this perspective and it will discount evidence that goes against it. If you think your life is predestined and hopeless, you will bring your worldview to life. You will think, "Why try anything? Why pray? Why bother? Nothing will change."

We've all known those people who seem mired in negative self-talk and a gloomy view of life. They are stuck in the past, unable to forgive and forget, stuck in images of themselves as unworthy. And, usually, their perspectives become self-fulfilling prophecies as their lives become mirror images of the negative affirmations they feed themselves every day.

Your belief system can either paralyze or empower you. Use your mind to create the world you want. Actively create your existence by what you think, say, feel, and do.

Great Things Come from Small Beginnings

One summer, a woman named Leslie visited Quetzeltenango, Guatemala, to participate in a three-week Spanish language immersion program. While there, she was overwhelmed by the poverty and the complete lack of medical aid she found in the post-civil war highlands. After watching a funeral procession for a three-year-old child who had died of a throat infection (easily treatable with simple antibiotics), she vowed to do something. While Leslie wasn't sure what form that action would take, her belief system was that when you put out your intention and step forward in faith, what you need will come to you.

She began by asking her pastor to allow her to give a talk about the need in that part of the world. To her amazement, doctors, nurses, and all sorts of people came up to her afterward, suggesting that they put together a group of medical workers to go to Guatemala. This humble beginning snowballed into Xela Aid, a not-for-profit humanitarian organization that has built a medical clinic and school in the village of San Martin Chiquito (their base of operations), has received millions of dollars worth of medical supplies and, over the last eight years, has treated thousands of local people. Far from just giving "handouts," this organization has empowered this Mayan village to help themselves in many ways, such as selling their handwoven crafts in the U.S. and microbanking locally. In fact, during the recent hurricane in Guatemala, San Martin Chiquito served as a base to distribute food, blankets, and medical aid to villagers in the area.

Great things come from small beginnings and belief in oneself and God. Think of your 21-day journal as a wise friend whispering in your ear, asking you questions to help you connect with your soul, find your life purpose, and set attainable goals. Even if you are passing through a time of discouragement or self-doubt, know that if you invest the time it takes daily to move through this journal, you will find it easier and easier to think positively, to feel clearer about your goals, and to understand the steps you can take to reach them. Not only that, but you will find yourself becoming energized in a way you never have before.

The first step toward empowerment is always faith, but remember what the Bible promises: "Ask and it will be given to you; seek and you will find; knock and the door will be opened to you." (Luke 11:9)

DREAM

I believe the universe is friendly because:

_____

_____

_____

One time that I felt everything in my life fit together perfectly was:

_____

_____

_____

The greatest kindness I remember was when:

_____

_____

_____

One person who had a great positive influence in my life was:

_____

_____

_____

I felt the most powerful and positive when:

_____

_____

_____

I know there is good in the world because:

_____

_____

_____

DEFINE

I want to live in a world that is:

_____

_____

_____

DO

One thing I could do to make my worldview real is:

_____

_____

_____

Day 2

Dream BIG

"I tell you the truth, if you have faith as small as a mustard seed, you can say to this mountain, 'Move from here to there' and it will move. Nothing will be impossible for you."
Matthew 17:20 (NIV)

If you knew that anything was possible in God, what would you do? What would you ask for? How would you live? How would you walk? What would you be able to perceive? What would you be able to see beyond?

Having a goal bigger than yourself is powerful. It redefines your existence. Every fiber of your being will be alive with purpose. Work, life, and love blend together. It all becomes good. Obstacles melt away—you walk through them. Allies seem to surface from all fronts. Resources become available where there were none before.

Why?

Because your success glorifies God. Living a rich life is what you were destined to do. Your Source Power wants you to succeed. When I declared my personal mission of economically empowering women worldwide, I could never have imagined the result. I found myself magically connecting with the perfect people to pursue the mission. For example, I wondered about the connection between fiscal health and physical health and needed a knowledgeable expert to review the book to flesh out this concept. Within a couple days of recognizing this need, I met Kathryn Linehan, creator of faith-oriented rotational movement (FORM). She facilitated a FORM exercise workshop at my church. I originally thought it was an accident that I showed up for the workshop an hour before the intended start time.

When Kathryn cited research from one of the *Fast Company* articles on change that I had used in this book, I knew she and I were on the same page. I approached her after the session to see if she would take a chance and review my manuscript. I learned that not only was she an expert on the connection between the spiritual and physical realm (as demonstrated through creating FORM), but she had also worked for years in the finance industry and could look at the manuscript through the eyes of a financial expert. She was the perfect editor.

We immediately connected on a soul level when I told her about the book idea and asked her to read through it and give me feedback. I dropped off the 150-page manuscript the next day and she added her wisdom throughout the book, generously donating her time, even though she was busy launching an exercise video series and had become involved in a global AIDS relief effort.

These "coincidences" in my life, where God sends help but chooses to remain anonymous, appear to be happening over and over again now.

So dream big. No excuses. We're not getting any younger, and the world is waiting for you to arrive. No dainty dreams. Think majestic. Draw your thoughts in bold colors. Cut out pictures of what you want to do, be, have, hold, and share. Spell it out in big block letters or swirling cursive script. Think back to your childhood. What did you dream about? If you can't remember, ask someone who knows you best or knew you back then. What did you talk about? What made you excited? What did you want to do? What did you want to be? What did you want to give to the world?

It takes courage to articulate your desires. Give yourself permission to do so. Do it—whether you believe your dreams will be fulfilled or not. Do it as if you had perfect conviction and faith that what you write down, draw, or cut out will be accomplished. Articulating it is the first act toward accomplishing it. By practicing, you will become more perfectly what God wants you to be: yourself.

Think this is selfish? It's not. Remember, this is not about you. It's about God. It's about living up to your potential. It's about living the fullest life that God meant for you. A little voice inside your head might be saying this is silly or conceited. That's not the voice of your loving God. It's a by-product of being brought up in this world. It's not your true voice. It's not your true calling. Remind yourself of the wise words of Marianne Williamson: "We ask ourselves, Who am I to be brilliant, gorgeous, talented, fabulous? Actually, who are you *not* to be? You are a child of God. Your playing small does not serve the world."

Start journaling by considering these questions:

DREAM

What desires keep coming up in my life?

_____

_____

_____

What matters most to me?

_____

_____

_____

What fills me full of joy?

_____

_____

_____

What qualities do I admire most in others?

_____

_____

_____

DEFINE

How do I really want to live my life?

_____

_____

_____

What gives my life passion and purpose?

_____

_____

_____

What do I want to be remembered for?

_____

_____

_____

If I knew I could accomplish anything in God, what would I do?

_____

_____

_____

DO

I will commit to working toward fulfilling this personal mission:
I, _____, am here to make the world
a better place by _____,
and by doing so, I will see the following result(s):

_____

_____

_____

One action I can take to start living my personal mission is to:

_____

_____

DAY 3

DISCOVER YOUR STRENGTHS

There is only one you. You were equipped with magnificent qualities, talents, strengths, and skills all wrapped up in a unique personality. Truly living a rich life means using your gifts to help others.

You have only so much time on this planet. Living a selfish existence is not useful, meaningful, or fulfilling. It's unsatisfying because you were meant to share yourself with the world. Service and significance go hand in hand. Rick Warren calls the custom combination that God equips you with as your SHAPE, which stands for:

- **S**piritual gifts—God-empowered abilities for serving Him
- **H**eart—what you care about; your passions
- **A**bilities—natural talents you were born with
- **P**ersonality—characteristics of you as a person
- **E**xperience—what you've lived through

The sooner you recognize what God has given you, the sooner you can get on with living a rich life. To discover your strengths, consider the statements and questions on the following pages.

DREAM

I've always been told I'm good at:

_____

_____

_____

I have a gift for:

_____

_____

_____

I get excited when I:

_____

_____

_____

I love:

_____

_____

_____

People who know me best use the following words to describe me:

_____

_____

_____

What I like most about myself is:

_____

_____

_____

When I succeed, most often it's because of:

_____

_____

_____

These experiences most define my life:

_____

_____

_____

What have I lived through that I can use to help others?

_____

_____

_____

DEFINE

I would describe my SHAPE as:

Spiritual gifts:

_____

Heart:

_____

Abilities:

_____

Personality:

_____

Experience:

_____

DO

One thing I could do to use my SHAPE to help others is:

_____

_____

_____

DAY 4

BANISH BAD BELIEFS

"Be careful how you think: your life is shaped by your thoughts."
Proverbs 4:23 (TEV)

Was journaling over the last three days difficult? Did you find that unwelcome thoughts and self-doubts filled your head? Did you hear things like "that's silly," "who do you think you are?" and "you can't do that"? That's called the monkey mind.

The monkey mind is that nonproductive daily chatter going on inside our heads that keeps us from living a focused life. In the jungle of daily distractions, the monkey mind delights in swinging from thought to thought and disrupting our peace of mind. Just as we're about to undertake something positive and powerful, our monkey mind sabotages our success by introducing negative thoughts, beliefs, or feelings dredged up from the past or present. Taming the monkey mind takes focus and refraining from judgment. To render it powerless, we need to call out that voice and catalog what it's saying. By identifying what's standing in the way, we can prepare our minds to accept more positive beliefs.

Find a comfortable place. Sit down and close your eyes. Take in a deep breath and ask God into your presence. Exhale and let go of all the tension, frustration, fear, and judgment you may have inside. Breathe out all your need to condemn or find fault with yourself. Breathe in all the love, compassion, and peace in the universe—an unlimited supply available through connection with your Source Power.

For the first thirty-nine years of her life, Shelly had labored under the false belief that she was worthless and didn't deserve

119

wealth. She found herself going bankrupt more than once and constantly moving from one financial catastrophe to another. Shelly was a magnet for money melodrama until she began to meditate on all the many blessings and gifts she truly had. Slowly, she let go of feeling worthless by asking for God's guidance and requesting that He use her in a more powerful, purposeful way. Shelly reframed how she looked at her wealth, switching from seeing money as the key to personal fulfillment to viewing money as an abundant resource to enable her to do good in the world. She miraculously landed a new job with a six-figure salary and began to attract peaceful and productive interactions in her family relationships, at home, and at the office.

Start to listen for your inner voice. As soon as you begin listening for it, your monkey mind will start acting up. Be strong. You can defeat it by outlasting it. Start writing down the negative thoughts, words, and beliefs that surface, and label them as barriers to genius. Write whatever comes to mind, or if you're stuck, use the statements and questions below to dispel the poison.

DREAM

What is most unfair in the world is:

_____

_____

_____

I was told as a child that:

_____

_____

_____

When I fail, it's most often because:

_____

_____

_____

Obstacles I must face are:

_____

_____

_____

DEFINE

What do I believe about myself, both good and bad?

_____

_____

_____

What do I fear most?

_____

_____

_____

DO

On a piece of paper, write down all the beliefs that have held you back that you've acquired from others throughout your life. Go to your fireplace or barbecue or other safe area and light the paper on fire. Watch it burn and say out loud: "I no longer hold self-limiting beliefs." If you find the same negative beliefs resurfacing, repeat this act and replace the old beliefs with new, positive ones by making a new commitment.

Say out loud: "I realize that I attract what I focus my mind on. From today forward, I will focus on my purpose." Your word is your most powerful tool of creation. By declaring what you want, you set the universe in motion to deliver on your declaration. If you make your declaration in front of others, you engage their support in keeping you accountable. God created the world by speaking it into existence. God imagined what the world would be like, and through His word, God created it. Your word is holy and powerful. Use it in a positive way.

My purpose or goal is:

_____

_____

_____

My intention is:

_____

_____

_____

Start each day by standing in front of the mirror and reciting your purpose and intention. Pray for God's help in fulfilling these two things.

DAY 5

REALIGN

"God is our refuge and strength, an ever-present help in trouble. Therefore we will not fear, though the earth give way and the mountains fall into the heart of the sea, though its waters roar and foam and the mountains quake with their surging."
Psalm 46:1–3 (NIV)

Nothing is impossible with God. The size of your God determines the size of your goals. How big is your God?

They say that the bedrock of what we believe about God is based on our relationship with our parents or caretakers. If our parents were fair and loving, we tend to believe God is fair and loving. If our parents were unloving and unforgiving, we tend to believe that God is such. Although we learn about God through our own spiritual experiences and exposure to church, sometimes those unmet childhood needs can color our relationship with God. When you bring these beliefs to light, you can examine them and see if they are affecting your ability to connect with God.

Although she was a smart, capable woman, Joann was a procrastinator. She always put off doing what she knew was good for her. Always last in line, eating the scraps off her children's plates, Joann had a belief that she didn't matter and didn't deserve the good things in life. However, Joann was able to become aware of this belief through a WorldWorks transformational workshop where she examined both her relationship with her mother and the underlying events in her life that had shaped her belief about being unworthy. The root of this belief for Joann was witnessing her mother being beaten and verbally abused by her father. Once Joann uncovered and acknowledged this belief, released it, and forgave her mother and father, she was able to create a new empowering belief in herself as being infinitely worthy to live a happy, joyous life. Her new belief opened up the possibility of investing in herself by pursuing an education and establishing a lucrative career as an accountant.

DREAM

What was your relationship with your parents like?

_____

_____

_____

What did you enjoy about your parents?

_____

_____

_____

What hurts did you experience as a child?

_____

_____

_____

What needs went unmet?

_____

_____

_____

How did you learn about God?

_____

_____

_____

What do you believe about God?

_____

_____

_____

How would you describe God?

_____

_____

_____

DEFINE

What is your relationship with God?

_____

_____

_____

What do you expect from God?

_____

_____

_____

How has God worked in your life?

_____

_____

_____

DO

Have a God moment each day. Find quiet time to pray. God wants a relationship with you, so don't edge Him out. Invest a couple moments each day alone to:

1. Thank God for at least one thing in your life
2. Tell God what's in your heart
3. Ask for help for others and for yourself

DAY 6

FORGIVE

"If we confess our sins, he is faithful and just and will forgive us our sins and purify us from all unrighteousness."
1 John 1:9 (NIV)

A cancer that most of us carry around with us is past hurts. People are imperfect. Parents are imperfect. Spouses, children, friends, neighbors, coworkers, you name it—all of us make mistakes. We hurt others and we get hurt. That's life. But the difference between living richly and living in spiritual poverty is developing the ability to forgive those past hurts and move on.

God is perfect. In God, all things are possible, including forgiveness. To embrace a rich life, we need to unburden ourselves of negativity. We all need to forgive—to let go of what was done in the past and release ourselves from the bondage of bitterness so we can embrace wealth. Forgiveness benefits you more than the person you forgive. By forgiving, you set yourself free.

If you have never experienced a hurt, you can skip past this daily reflection. However, most of us *have* been hurt, and a lot of us hold on to old hurts even years after they have occurred, until, like unclean wounds, they fester and scar us.

Our ability to forgive is equal to how forgiven we feel. If you don't feel forgiven by God, you can't extend forgiveness to yourself or to others. To begin unburdening yourself of past hurts, consider the statements on the following pages.

DREAM

The things that have hurt me most in my life are:

_____

_____

_____

The people who caused me the most pain are:

_____

_____

_____

If I could change one thing in my life, it would be:

_____

_____

_____

DEFINE

The one thing in my life I can't get over is:

_____

_____

_____

DO

I will repeatedly follow this process when a past hurt comes to my mind:

1. I will strive to forgive the person who hurt me. Letting go of past hurts and bitterness may take time, but I know that it will be worth it, since living without forgiveness is a heavy burden.
2. I will pray for God to help that person and to help me move on.
3. I will remember that harboring negative feelings hurts me most of all and keeps me from living a happy life.
4. I will not be bitter. I know that this hurt will heal and make me stronger and that God will use my hurt for a greater purpose.

Day 7

Stop Worrying

"With God's power working in us, God can do much, much more than anything we can ask or imagine."
Ephesians 3:20 (NCV)

You attract what you most focus on. If you are a worrier, you attract what you worry about. In order to accomplish anything in life, you need to stop worrying. It's a big time and energy suck. It keeps you stuck in the past or future and doesn't allow you to get on with the present.

Worrying is overrated. God will give you only what you can handle. God will provide what you need. Trusting God will build your faith. Building your faith will fuel your success. Bring all your worries to God and let Him deal with them.

From here forward, you are not allowed to worry. When you feel a worry coming over you, you are to say aloud, "No, I won't worry about that." If life has dealt you a blow, remember that God is here for you and pray about your concern. God delights in taking all your burdens and carrying them for you.

When Joy was diagnosed with breast cancer, she used it as an opportunity to become a spiritual athlete. Cancer patients have every right to feel self-pity, but Joy became a beacon of physical transcendence and wrote about her experience in her book *Radiant Warrior*. Sharing her story of pain and triumph glorified God and lightened her load. Meanwhile, Joy shone a light for all cancer patients to walk a path of peace and purpose, helping them to embrace the belief that they had freely chosen their journey through cancer to help them develop as a human being and uplift their fellow humans.

If you are tired or worried all the time, you won't have the strength to accomplish all the wonderful things that God wants you to do. So quit fretting over the big and small things. Assign them to God.

DREAM

I most worry about:

_____

_____

_____

My worrying accomplishes:

_____

_____

_____

Focusing on my worries hurts me because:

_____

_____

_____

DEFINE

My biggest fear is:

_____

_____

_____

DO

When I feel worry coming on, I will:

1. Say to myself: "No, I will not worry." I will repeat this until my mind quiets down.
2. Pray to God: "I am not going to worry, because you will handle this."
3. Remember that God works all things for good for those who love Him and for those who are called according to His purpose.
4. Do something constructive instead, such as volunteering for some charity work, giving a friend or family member a helping hand, doing something kind for a young person or elder, or doing something I really love, such as taking a walk in nature.

DAY 8

CONDUCT A SPIRITUAL CHECKUP

"Delight yourself in the Lord and He will give you the desires of your heart."

Psalm 37:4 (NIV)

Open up and say "aaahhh." It's time to give yourself a checkup to find out where you are in the five fields of endeavor: spiritual, emotional, mental, physical, and fiscal. We start with the spiritual because that's the source of everything else.

Spirit means "breathe." It's what distinguishes us from corpses. We have life in us. And the state of that life affects every other aspect of our lives: how emotionally stable we are, how mentally fit we are, how physically fit we are, and how fiscally blessed we are.

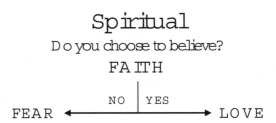

Your spirit is most like God. It's pure light, transcendent, eternal. Without it, your body will wither and die. Your wealth will come and go. Your mental and emotional states will change with the weather or the state of your digestion. But your spirit endures. It's like the Energizer Bunny®, only it doesn't need batteries. It craves connection to God.

Your faith determines the state of your spirit. The stronger your faith, the stronger your spirit will be and the more you will choose to live in love. The stronger your spirit, the more you will be able to reject fear.

Perform the following spiritual checkup:

DREAM

If I died today, God would say to me:

_____

_____

_____

If I died today, my one regret would be:

_____

_____

_____

I would describe my spirit as:

_____

_____

_____

What I crave most is:

_____

_____

_____

My spiritual vision of life is:

_____

_____

_____

I would characterize my praying as:

_____

_____

_____

I seek God by:

_____

_____

_____

DEFINE

I feel closest to God when I:

_____

_____

_____

DO

Strengthening your spirit can be accomplished by making a practice of:

- **Meditating.** God comes to the quiet mind. In the middle of life's distractions, it's hard to get a spiritual connection. Make time each day to spend quiet time alone so you can recharge your spirit. Lisa, a reality television show director, brought clarity and peace to her hectic life by meditating at least five minutes a day. The pressure of production schedules and accommodating difficult personalities melted away as she infused herself with purpose. As Lisa became more centered, she was led to find more meaningful work that nourished her soul. She began directing the types of programs that aligned with her value system and inspired viewers.

- **Praying.** Talk to God on a daily basis. Express what you are thankful for, as well as what's in your heart—your needs and desires. Ask how you can be of service to others. Ask to become more aware of the opportunities that abound for helping those around you and making the world a better place. Ask for help.

- **Reading.** The Bible contains all of God's promises and speaks to every concern. Read it and your faith will grow. Read spiritual books. Listen to inspired music. Your mind is prime real estate. Be careful what you put into it.
- **Connecting.** Find people who nourish your faith. God speaks to you through people. God helps you through people. Surround yourself with genuinely spiritual folks.

To strengthen my spirit, I commit to the following actions:

_____

_____

_____

DAY 9

CONDUCT AN EMOTIONAL CHECKUP

Unlike your spirit, your emotions will change from day to day. They will vary in intensity and mood. The strength of your emotional state can be measured by your peace of mind. If you find yourself constantly flying off the handle, chances are you are worrying about something that is robbing you of your peace of mind.

Your emotional state is extremely important because it drives your decision making. Without an emotional impetus, it's impossible to make a decision. We would continue in an endless loop of evaluation and never come to a conclusion. There would always be more calculations to be done and more evaluation needed. You could never be 100 percent sure that your decision would totally optimize all the variables in a situation.

However, when you are clearly passionate about achieving a goal, you enjoy the journey and achieve results seemingly without effort. For example, Shannon wanted to sharpen her yoga skills by learning from the masters in India. Plane ticket in hand, she emotionally knew what she wanted to do, even though she didn't logically know how it would all unfold. Miraculously, Shannon met the perfect people to help her actualize her trip. Opportunities presented themselves for her to spend three months trekking across India, studying with gurus, and bathing in the Ganges. She said this journey worked out even better than she could have imagined.

It's vitally important to check in on your emotional state. To get a "feel" for where you are emotionally, complete the statements on the following pages.

Spiritual
Do you choose to believe?

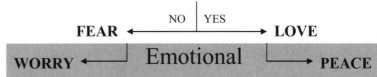

FAITH

NO | YES

FEAR ← → **LOVE**

WORRY ← Emotional → **PEACE**

DREAM

The emotion that most dominates my life is:

_____

_____

_____

I feel most peaceful when I:

_____

_____

_____

I feel most out of control when I:

_____

_____

_____

I worry most about:

_____

_____

_____

DEFINE

When I "lose it," it's most often because:

_____

_____

_____

DO

To improve your emotional state, invest in yourself by:

- **Resting.** Most often, we run ourselves ragged. We're in constant motion thinking that the world is going to stop if we stop. Give yourself a rest. Don't carry the world on your shoulders. Start by getting enough sleep. Plan relaxing activities every day, such as meditating, being in nature, or taking minibreaks during which you close your eyes and "visit" one of your favorite places in your imagination.
- **Assigning.** Write a daily list for God of the things you would like Him to help you with. Remember, you are not in this alone. You have the powers of the universe at your beck and call. If you devote your life to God and live for His purpose, He will be there to meet your needs. Trust enough to assign

to Him the burdens in your life. He will take care of them.

- **Refocusing.** Nearly 90 percent of what we focus on in life will have no lasting consequences. On a daily basis, we're preoccupied with what laundry detergent to buy, what to cook for dinner, who said what about whom, etc.—stuff that is meaningless under the lens of eternity. If that's the case, then not sweating the small stuff takes on a different light. When we do not struggle to optimize every facet of our existence, we free ourselves to focus on our real purpose and do things that make the world a better place for our family, ourselves, our community, our country, and our world.

Amanda demanded perfection. She micromanaged her staff, husband, family, and friends. Her upbringing had taught her to be strong and not reveal her vulnerability. Because of this, her heart was an impenetrable fortress to which even she herself did not have access. Her mantra was that it is better to be envied than liked. Then she had a car accident and found herself in the hospital, near death. For the first time in her life, Amanda had to rely on God and the kindness of others for her recovery. She learned to let go and let God. As a result, Amanda reframed life as a gift. She learned to cherish every moment with her family and friends. The death of her obsession with micromanagement resulted in the birth of her freedom, joy, and peace.

To improve my emotional state, I commit to doing the following on a daily basis:

_____

_____

_____

DAY 10

CONDUCT A MENTAL CHECKUP

"Trust in the Lord with all your heart; do not depend on your own understanding. Seek His will in all you do, and He will direct your paths."

Proverbs 3:5–6 (NLT)

The more of a control freak you are, the more unstable your mental state is going to be. From an early age, we are taught to depend on ourselves, and we are told that we are responsible for many things outside our control—mainly the happiness or material condition of others. As children, we assume these responsibilities because it makes us feel as if we have some control, that we have the power to make things better. But that's only partially true.

We never did have and never will have control over the actions of others. It's not our responsibility to make other people happy. Our responsibility is only to live for God's purpose. Everyone's happiness is their individual responsibility—not ours.

I have a friend who used to expend tremendous amounts of energy trying to "fix" the people around her so that they would be happy and able to solve their problems. Not surprisingly, none of her efforts ever really worked and she ended up exhausted and emotionally frustrated. When she finally woke up, stopped trying to control everyone by changing them, and focused on the things she *could* change in *her own* life, not only was she happier, but to her amazement, everyone else around her was happier and better off as well. The reason for this was that by trying to control everyone's destiny by "helping" them, she was hindering the important life lessons they needed to learn by solving their own problems.

Another important point to remember is that it is unhealthy and futile to try and live your life to please others. If you try and live this way, you will never win. Everything is possible in God, but God's goals don't include making everyone happy all the time.

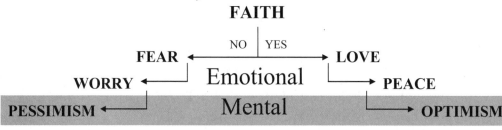

Spiritual
Do you choose to believe?
FAITH

The strength of your mental state is measured by how optimistic you are. Complete these statements to check your mental health:

DREAM

I tend to think of life as:

_____

_____

_____

My first reaction when I encounter a problem is:

_____

_____

_____

I define failure as:

_____

_____

_____

I define success as:

_____

_____

_____

I feel like anything is possible when I:

_____

_____

_____

I feel hopeless when I:

_____

_____

_____

I ask for God's help when:

_____

_____

_____

DEFINE

The biggest problem in my life that I've overcome is:

_____

_____

_____

The things that helped me overcome this problem were:

_____

_____

_____

DO

The key to a positive state of mind is perspective and resourcefulness. Problems will always be a part of life, but we certainly have it within our power to change the way we view and react to them, not letting them deplete our energy through needless worry. To expand your mind takes mental gymnastics. The following actions help build mental muscles:

- **Help others.** You don't know that God is all you need until God is all you've got. Go learn that from others. Find a mission, cause, or volunteer organization to support. By helping someone less fortunate, you'll see how God has blessed you. Find out the true meaning of resourcefulness by listening to the story of someone who has survived on the streets.

  On a flight from Orange County, California, to Dallas, Texas, Linda got to know a stripper named Asia. Asia said that she chose to be a stripper as a quick way to get money and to overcome her association between sexual expression and being molested as a child. An affluent housewife and mother, Linda had never been in a strip club and had never gone hungry a day in her life. On that flight, Linda learned that there was little difference between her and Asia and that under similar circumstances, she might have made the same choices. Asia's story touched her soul and, as a result of this chance meeting, Linda began to do outreach at women's shelters.

- **Ask for the lesson.** When a problem emerges or tragedy strikes, ask God what you are supposed to learn from this. God truly does work everything for good. That doesn't mean that all things are good, but that God *uses* them for good. Think about your greatest weakness, greatest shame, or greatest hurt. If you give that to God, He will use it for His glory. He'll allow you to take what you've learned from that experience, reach out and connect with another, and use that knowledge to turn around a life. For example, I have a friend who is a breast cancer survivor. Going through cancer treatments for a year was the most physically and emotionally painful experience of her life, yet it was also her greatest spiritual triumph as she opened herself up to God's love and to the support of the friends and family members around her. Now that she is well, she is able to take what she learned from this illness and use it to help others going through health and life challenges.

- **Adopt an attitude of gratitude.** Count your blessings. Catalog them. Carry them to God and say thank you. Your health is a blessing. Your body is a blessing. Your life is a gift. Live in the present as if you're unwrapping a present from your best friend.

I commit to improving my mental state by doing the following on a daily basis:

_____

_____

_____

DAY 11

CONDUCT A PHYSICAL CHECKUP

Medical experts are uncovering more and more evidence that our physical condition is linked to the way we think and what we believe. Our body is the temple of God. If our body is run down, diseased, or depressed, we'll have a tougher time accomplishing our purpose on the planet.

God meant for us to enjoy our body. He created it for us to have fun in. We experience the world through what we see, what we hear, what we touch, what we smell, and what we taste. Keeping up our health not only helps us do things, but also improves our enjoyment of life. No one can really enjoy their work, family, or leisure time if they are struggling with (avoidable) health problems such as type 2 diabetes, heart disease, addiction to alcohol or pharmaceuticals (legal or illegal), and joints worn out by obesity. The old adage that you have everything if you have your health is true today more than ever.

Our physical state is measured by how healthy we feel. To assess your health, complete the statements on the following pages.

Spiritual
Do you choose to believe?
FAITH

NO | YES

FEAR ← | → LOVE

WORRY ← | Emotional | → PEACE

PESSIMISM ← | Mental | → OPTIMISM

WEAKNESS ← | Physical | → STRENGTH

DREAM

I felt the strongest in my life when I:

_____

_____

_____

I felt the weakest in my life when I:

_____

_____

_____

My current state of health is:

_____

_____

_____

What I like most about my body is:

_____

_____

_____

I tend to get sick when I:

_____

_____

_____

I have the following health challenges:

_____

_____

_____

I take care of myself by:

_____

_____

_____

How much I exercise:

_____

_____

_____

What I eat:

_____

_____

_____

How much I sleep:

_____

_____

_____

DEFINE

Taking better care of myself would allow me to:

_____

_____

_____

DO

Investing in your health is not a selfish endeavor. The better you feel physically, the more positive your outlook will be, the more you'll have to give to others, the better able you'll be to take care of yourself and others, and the more impact you'll have on the planet. Invest in your health by:

- **Thinking about those you love.** You are an important person. You touch the lives of so many people. The world wants you to be around and wants to enjoy what you have to offer. Don't cut your life short by neglecting your health.

- **Taking advantage of preventive care benefits.** If you have health insurance, it usually covers physicals, prescreenings, and tests at 100 percent or for a small copayment. Treat a condition early and you can most often cure it. Let it go and little stuff can kill you.

- **Walking in nature and talking to God.** Each day, spend some time in nature. Go for a half-hour walk. Talk to God. Get everything off your chest. It will improve your spirit and your health.

- **Investing in lifestyle changes that bring big returns,** such as practicing good nutrition, exercising wisely, and getting restful sleep. Some good books that offer program guidelines in nutrition, exercise, and health management are *Turn Up the Heat* by Philip L. Goglia and *Maximum Energy for Life* and *The Fat-Burning Bible* by Mackie Shilstone.

DAY 12

CONDUCT A FISCAL CHECKUP

Your fiscal state is the outward sign of your spiritual, emotional, mental, and physical states. What's in your bank account isn't as important as what you *think* about your fiscal state. You may have millions but still live a worried existence—feverishly working for more and more, thinking that money is what you need to feel secure. You may have little money but worry little because you know that God is your true source of wealth. You know that God will provide for all your needs.

One measure of fiscal health is your level of contentment with what you have. Remembering that you need God in the midst of material wealth is difficult. The more you have, the more likely you will be living with the illusion that you are independent and self-sufficient. And the more you set yourself apart, the more spiritually impoverished you will become.

Spiritual

Do you choose to believe?

FAITH

	NO	YES	
FEAR ←		→	LOVE
WORRY ←	**Emotional**	→	PEACE
PESSIMISM ←	**Mental**	→	OPTIMISM
WEAKNESS ←	**Physical**	→	STRENGTH
HUNGER ←	**Fiscal**	→	CONTENTMENT

Check your fiscal state by completing the statements below:

DREAM

My first money memory is:

_____

_____

_____

How I handle money can best be characterized as:

_____

_____

_____

My biggest money problem is:

_____

_____

_____

The biggest financial lesson I have to learn is:

_____

_____

_____

I feel out of control financially when I:

_____

_____

_____

I define rich as:

_____

_____

_____

I feel most content when I:

_____

_____

_____

When I give to others, I feel:

_____

_____

_____

I feel I'm providing for my family when:

_____

_____

_____

DEFINE

My greatest wealth is:

_____

_____

_____

DO

Growing your wealth can be accomplished in three ways: by increasing your level of contentment with what you have, by increasing your resources, or by more wisely using the resources you have. All of these actions have more to do with how you *feel* about wealth than with the actual amount of money you have. More than half the world lives on less than $2.50 a day, which in their economies translates into not enough, or barely enough, to survive. So, if you are earning enough to survive with some extra left over, ask yourself two questions:

1. Are you using your wealth in a way that God would be proud of?
2. Do you truly appreciate how fortunate you are?

I commit to doing the following on a daily basis to better appreciate and use my resources:

_____

_____

_____

Day 13

Discover a Promise

"Those who hope in the Lord will renew their strength. They will soar on wings like eagles; they will run and not grow weary, they will walk and not be faint."

Isaiah 40:31 (NIV)

God doesn't want you to go it alone. Whatever you go after in His name, you will have resources, strength, and comfort as God has promised. God wants you to achieve big things. He wants to help you get there.

When things get difficult, when you encounter the inevitable obstacles, when something goes wrong, find a promise that speaks to you. Memorize it. Recite it to yourself when the going gets tough.

There are more than seven thousand promises in the Bible. Here are some to help you in your journey.

SPIRITUAL

Faith

"Without faith, no one can please God. Anyone who comes to God must believe that He is real and that He rewards those who truly want to find him." Hebrews 11:6 (NCV)

"For everyone born of God overcomes the world. This is the victory that has overcome the world, even our faith." 1 John 5:4 (NIV)

"I tell you the truth, if you have faith as small as a mustard seed, you can say to this mountain, 'Move from here to there' and it will move. Nothing will be impossible for you." Matthew 17:20 (NIV)

"Being confident of this, that he who began a good work in you will carry it on to completion until the day of Christ Jesus." Philippians 1:6 (NIV)

Fear

"When you go through deep waters and great trouble, I will be with you. When you go through rivers of difficulty, you will not drown! When you walk through the fire of oppression, you will not be burned up; the flames will not consume you. " Isaiah 43:2

Purpose

"I am the vine; you are the branches. If a man remains in me and I in him, he will bear much fruit; apart from me you can do nothing." John 15:5 (NIV)

Temptation

"But remember that the temptations that come into your life are no different from what others experience. And God is faithful. He will keep the temptation from becoming so strong that you can't stand up against it. When you are tempted, he will show you a way out so that you will not give in to it." 1 Corinthians 10:13 (NLT)

EMOTIONAL

Comfort

"Praise be to the God and Father of our Lord Jesus Christ, the Father of compassion and the God of all comfort, who comforts us in all our troubles, so that we can comfort those in any trouble with the comfort we ourselves have received from God." 2 Corinthians 1:3–4 (NIV)

Loneliness

"God makes a home for the lonely. He leads out the prisoners into prosperity; only the rebellious dwell in a parched land." Psalm 68:6 (NASB)

"Be happy with what you have because God has said, 'I will never abandon you or leave you.'" Hebrews 13:5b (GW)

Worry

"Do not be anxious about anything, but in everything, by prayer and petition, with thanksgiving, present your requests to God. And the peace of God, which transcends all understanding, will guard your hearts and your minds in Christ Jesus." Philippians 4:6–7 (NIV)

Forgiveness

"Repent therefore and return, that your sins may be wiped away, in order that times of refreshing may come from the presence of the Lord." Acts 3:19 (NASB)

Despair

"We are hard pressed on every side, but not crushed; perplexed, but not in despair; persecuted, but not abandoned; struck down, but not destroyed." 2 Corinthians 4:8–9 (NIV)

MENTAL

Wisdom

"If any of you lacks wisdom, he should ask God, who gives generously to all without finding fault, and it will be given to him." James 1:5 (NIV)

Confusion

"Trust in the Lord with all your heart; do not depend on your own understanding. Seek His will in all you do, and He will direct your paths." Proverbs 3:5–6 (NLT)

Obstacles

"Not only so, but we also rejoice in our sufferings, because we know that suffering produces perseverance; perseverance, character; and character, hope." Romans 5:3–4 (NIV)

PHYSICAL

Strength

"Those who hope in the Lord will renew their strength. They will soar on wings like eagles; they will run and not grow weary, they will walk and not be faint." Isaiah 40:31 (NIV)

"My flesh and my heart may fail, but God is the strength of my heart and my portion forever." Psalm 73:26 (NIV)

Rest

"Come to me, all you who are weary and burdened, and I will give you rest. Take my yoke upon you and learn from me, for I am gentle and humble in heart, and you will find rest for your souls." Matthew 11:28–29 (NIV)

FISCAL

Plan

"Commit to the Lord whatever you do, and your plans will succeed." Proverbs 16:3 (NIV)

Share

"Each one should give as you have decided in your heart to give. You should not be sad when you give, and you should not give because you feel forced to give. God loves the person who gives happily. And God can give you more blessings than you need. Then you will always have plenty of everything — enough to give to every good work." 2 Corinthians 9:7–8 (NCV)

"'Bring the whole tithe into the storehouse, that there may be food in my house. Test me on this,' says the Lord Almighty, 'and see if I will not throw open the floodgates of heaven and pour out so much blessing that you will not have room enough for it.'" Malachi 3:10 (NIV)

"Give, and it will be given to you. A good measure, pressed down, shaken together and running over, will be poured into your lap. For with the measure you use, it will be measured to you." Luke 6:38 (NIV)

Security

"God will supply all your needs from his riches in glory because of what Christ Jesus has done for us." Philippians 4:19

"He will give you all you need from day to day if you make the Kingdom of God your primary concern." Luke 12:31 (NLT)

DREAM

The promise I most need to hear now is:

_____

_____

_____

In order to fulfill my purpose, I need to believe that:

_____

_____

_____

DEFINE

How would my life change if I lived on God's promises?

_____

_____

_____

DO

Pick one promise. Memorize it. Remind yourself of it when you need it. Watch for evidence that God is delivering on that promise.

Lynn loved Romans 8:28: "And we know that all things work together for good to them who love God, to them that are called according to his purpose." When she started really believing and living this verse, Lynn's life changed. She trusted herself to channel God's inspiration through her art. She no longer feared selling her art and making the business connections necessary to get her works noticed and sold. Lynn let go of the need for perfection and the right conditions to create her art—she surrendered to the visions she received and allowed them to flow through her to take concrete form on her canvases. As a result, thousands of people were inspired by her example and bought her work.

DAY 14

DREAM BIG SPIRITUALLY

Now is the time to redefine your beliefs and your expectations and to unleash your creativity to redefine your **spiritual** life.

Use whatever creative medium is going to create the most permanent and perfect image in your mind of what you want to achieve. Articulate your intentions in words, drawings, photos, pictures, sounds, tastes, and experiences. Take this part of the journaling process as far as you can push it. The more senses you involve in the process of setting your goals, the more real your goals will become for you. For a sculptor, this means creating your image in clay, letting your hands create the world you want to experience. For a pianist, this means playing the music that most touches your soul and sparks the images of your ideal life. For a writer, this means creating a story of what you want your work, your family relationships, and your impact on the planet to be. Pick the medium that best expresses your inner thoughts.

Let your mind go wild in what you hope to accomplish spiritually. Consider these statements and questions:

DREAM

What does spiritual connection look like? Sound like? Feel like? Smell like? Taste like?

_____

_____

_____

How will I feel when I'm perfectly aligned with God's purpose?

_____

_____

_____

Other people will know I have a strong spirit by:

_____

_____

_____

How will my interactions with others be positively affected by my improved spirit?

_____

_____

_____

DEFINE

My spiritual goal is:

_____

_____

_____

DO

I will commit to the following to reach my spiritual goal:

_____

_____

_____

I will accomplish this goal by:

_____

_____

_____

I will measure my progress by:

_____

_____

_____

DAY 15

DREAM BIG EMOTIONALLY

In order to have a richer and more rewarding **emotional** life, it is necessary that you begin to redefine your beliefs and expectations and unleash your creativity.

Use whatever creative means is going to create the most permanent and perfect image in your mind of what you want to achieve. Articulate your intentions in words, drawings, photos, pictures, sounds, tastes, and experiences. Take this journaling process as far as you can push it. The more senses you involve in the process of setting your goals, the more real your goals will become for you.

Give your mind free reign in discovering what you hope to accomplish **emotionally**. Don't hold back, censor yourself, intellectualize, or judge. Start by considering these statements and questions:

DREAM

What does peace of mind look like? Sound like? Feel like? Smell like? Taste like?

_____

_____

_____

How will I feel when I'm perfectly emotionally aligned with God's purpose?

_____

_____

_____

Other people will know I have peace of mind by:

_____

_____

_____

How will my interactions with others be positively affected by my improved peace of mind?

_____

_____

_____

DEFINE

My emotional goal is:

_____

_____

_____

DO

I will commit to the following to reach my emotional goal:

_____

_____

_____

I will accomplish this goal by:

_____

_____

_____

I will measure my progress by:

_____

_____

_____

DAY 16

DREAM BIG MENTALLY

Here are some questions, guidelines, and exercises to help you redefine your **mental** life and learn how to dream big.

Again, allow yourself to use any and all creative means to create a permanent and perfect image in your mind of what you hope to achieve. Articulate your intentions in whatever ways serve you best: words, drawings, photos, pictures, sounds, tastes, and experiences. Don't hold back—take this journaling process as far as you can push it. The more senses you involve in the process of setting your goals, the more real your goals will become for you.

Let your mind be completely free to explore whatever you hope to accomplish **mentally**. Use the following statements and questions as a guide:

DREAM

What does a positive mental outlook look like? Sound like? Feel like? Smell like? Taste like?

_____

_____

_____

How will I feel when I'm mentally aligned with God's purpose?

_____

_____

_____

Other people will know I have a positive mental attitude by:

_____

_____

_____

How will my interactions with others be positively affected by my positive mental attitude?

_____

_____

_____

DEFINE

My mental goal is:

_____

_____

_____

DO

I will commit to the following to reach my mental goal:

_____

_____

_____

I will accomplish this goal by:

_____

_____

_____

I will measure my progress by:

_____

_____

_____

DAY 17

DREAM BIG PHYSICALLY

Throughout this book, I've been emphasizing the relationship between your **physical life** and your beliefs and expectations. This part of the journal is designed to help you unleash your creativity to create a healthier and more vibrant physical life.

Use whatever creative tools it takes to help you manifest the most permanent and perfect image in your mind of what you want to achieve physically. Continue to express your intentions in words, drawings, photos, pictures, sounds, tastes, and experiences. A great tool I would like you to consider is the movement-based Christian meditation practice called FORM—faith-oriented rotational movement. With FORM, you can learn how to integrate your breathing with stretching and strengthening movements that are performed while repeating inspirational verses from Psalm 23 and other scripture.

Kathryn Linehan, the creator of FORM, is a documentary filmmaker who also worked over 10 years in the financial field, helping families create their retirement assets and manage their wealth. Kathryn's mission is to help those who seek to live fully in their God-given potential. To read more about FORM, visit www.studioignite.com.

Take this process for dreaming big physically as far as you can push it, both through journal writing and embodying your dreams. The more senses you involve in the process of setting your goals, the more real your goals will become for you. Let your mind go wild in what you hope to accomplish **physically**.

Consider these statements and questions:

DREAM

What does perfect look like? Sound like? Feel like? Smell like? Taste like? Move like?

_____

_____

_____

How will I feel and breathe when I'm physically aligned with God's purpose?

_____

_____

_____

Other people will know I am healthy by:

_____

_____

_____

How will my interactions with others be positively affected by my improved health?

_____

_____

_____

DEFINE

My physical goal is:

_____

_____

_____

DO

I will commit to the following to reach my physical goal:

_____

_____

_____

I will accomplish this goal by:

_____

_____

_____

I will measure my progress by:

_____

_____

_____

DAY 18

DREAM BIG FISCALLY

Today you are going to apply all of the other lessons you've been learning to help you examine your beliefs and expectations and unleash your creativity to redefine your **fiscal** life.

As before, use whatever creative means—words, drawings, photos, pictures, sounds, tastes, and experiences—you wish to create a permanent and perfect image in your mind of what you want to achieve. Go for it! Remember, the more senses you can involve in this process of setting your goals, the more real your goals will become for you.

Let your mind go absolutely wild, freely expressing whatever you hope to accomplish **fiscally**. To help you achieve your goals, respond to the following statements and questions:

DREAM

What does real wealth look like? Sound like? Feel like? Smell like? Taste like?

_____

_____

_____

How will I feel when I'm growing my wealth and using it to further God's purpose?

_____

_____

_____

Other people will know I am content by:

_____

_____

_____

How will my interactions with others be positively affected by my improved wealth?

_____

_____

_____

DEFINE

My fiscal goal is:

_____

_____

_____

DO

I will commit to the following to reach my fiscal goal:

_____

_____

_____

I will accomplish this goal by:

_____

_____

_____

I will measure my progress by:

_____

_____

_____

Day 19

Plan to Succeed

So far during this journaling process, you've had a chance to thoroughly examine your beliefs, recognize your strengths, and imagine what you'd like to achieve spiritually, emotionally, mentally, physically, and fiscally. You've covered a lot of ground! Pat yourself on the back.

Now it's time to roll all your lessons, reflections, insights, and desires up into a master action plan. This doesn't have to be an overwhelming or tedious process. You can make this as detailed or big a picture as you'd like. The most important thing is to make a commitment to do *something* on a daily basis that gets you closer to your goal. This might include writing your goals out on paper and reflecting on them periodically. It is also important to track your progress and celebrate your success when you reach a milestone and fully accomplish your goal.

Remember, you're not in this alone. God hasn't just *made* you promises—He *acts* on those promises and speaks to you through the people He brings to your life. Watch for this.

Develop your master plan by considering the following:

DREAM

My purpose is:

_____

_____

_____

DEFINE

I can accomplish this purpose by aligning my intention with God's power and developing myself:

	My goal is:	My deadline is:	My measurement of success is:
Spiritually			
Emotionally			
Mentally			
Physically			
Fiscally			

DO

The only failure is giving up. I commit to working toward my goals in the following way:

	Daily Tasks	Monthly Check-In	Chart My Progress
Spiritually			
Emotionally			
Mentally			
Physically			
Fiscally			

DAY 20

BELIEVE IN ABUNDANCE

You are awash in resources. Your perspective brings those resources to light or hides them from view. Expectations become reality.

You get what you give.

Whatever you put out there comes back to you like a boomerang. If you approach the world with love, you will get love. If you invest time, money, energy in others, you will see a return on your investment. It may not come back to you in the form you expect, but it will come back to you. For example, Stacy never saw things as obstacles, only as opportunities. She was a master of creating win-wins wherever she went. Always the first to offer her love, time, and passion to encourage others, Stacy found herself on a trajectory headed straight for the C-suite at one of the world's most powerful bond companies. Her abundance flowed back to her in many forms—love, friendship, partnerships, and money. Stacy found that when she gave, she was the first to receive—tenfold.

Create your own abundance by considering the following:

DREAM

	What I most want:	What I am willing to give:
Spiritually		
Emotionally		
Mentally		
Physically		
Fiscally		

DEFINE

I know I live in abundance because:

_____

_____

_____

I see evidence of abundance in:

_____

_____

_____

I create my own abundance by:

_____

_____

_____

DO

Give what you want to receive:

_____

_____

_____

DAY 21

"BE TRANSFORMED
BY THE RENEWING OF YOUR MIND"

When I moved to California in 2001, I felt obligated to try yoga. When in Rome, do as the Romans. When in California, do yoga, preferably outdoors by a beach in the sunshine with your baby daughter. Five years later, I was introduced to the practice of FORM and learned how I could move and stretch with scripture. The practice of FORM is more than just exercise; it is a Bible study that involves ALL of me. I meditate on God's word, I breathe and move freely as the Spirit leads me, and best of all, I share this experience with my three-year-old son, Liam, and with other women. For the culmination of discovering your blessed life, we're going to do the FORM movement titled Abundance.

Abundance is the eighth exercise of FORM and teaches us to exhale and inhale while meditating on Psalm 23, verse 5: *"You anoint my head with oil; my cup overflows."* While sitting in a chair or on the floor, we exhale and round our entire torso to help us emphasize that we are pouring ourselves out completely, breathing out every last drop of air. While exhaling, we meditate on the phrase *"Anoint my head with oil,"* understanding that in order for us to be blessed, we must rely on God for inspiration and not move forward on our own seemingly good ideas.

As we wait for the impulse to inhale, we think about the next line in the Psalm, *"My cup overflows."* We may visualize how other lives become more blessed as we fulfill God's call in our own life. As we begin to inhale, we imagine the breath moving from the tailbone up one vertebra at a time to the base of the skull as we slowly straighten ourselves. During this slow inhalation and straightening, we find that as we sit taller, this posture embodies our seeking to be in alignment with God.

You can practice FORM right now—right where you are! Here's how:

1. Sit comfortably on a stable surface and feel where your hips and sit bones are situated. Make sure that your shoulders are squared and in alignment with your hips and let your head rest gently on your shoulders.

2. Exhale. Begin with bowing your head to release all tension as you round your neck, shoulders, thoracic region, and lower back. While you are exhaling, meditate on the scripture: *"You anoint my head with oil."* What does this mean to you today, right now in your life? You may want to journal and process what the Spirit is revealing to you today.

3. Inhale. Start with your tailbone, begin to sit taller, and straighten yourself one vertebra at a time until your hips, shoulders, and head feel as if a string is running through them and holding them one on top of the other. Do you feel as if your posture is more relaxed? While you are taking in this full breath, meditate on *"My cup overflows"* and remember all the lives that could be touched as you allow God's goodness to fill you and flow through you.

4. Repeat the breathing cycle ten times: exhale and round your spine, and then inhale and straighten your spine. To keep track of your breathing cycles, you can mark your movements by memorizing the fruit of the Spirit from Galatians 5:22–23: love, joy, peace, patience, kindness, goodness, faithfulness, gentleness, and self-control. Instead of counting from one to ten, count using the nine aspects of the fruit. Beginning and ending with love makes it ten!

As I learn to wait for my breath to lead the rounding and straightening of my back, I realize that embodying this scripture from Psalm 23 dramatically reinforces the principles of this book in a most powerful way. We hope the practice of FORM will open new possibilities for you to live the blessed life that you are destined to have. If you want to explore this further, there is a DVD for purchase on the FORM Web site.

Your Journey Begins!

Congratulations on undertaking your journey to discover your blessed life. Handling your finances is primarily an internal journey filled with worldly obstacles. Every obstacle you face is a form of fear—fear of not having enough, of being unloved, of not fitting in, of being overwhelmed, of losing control, of being invisible, of insignificance. But remember that every one of these obstacles is perfectly designed as an opportunity for you to break through your fears and experience your greatness.

Veronica was afraid of failure. Although she was a successful manager at a health care company, Veronica's real love was acting and writing. Her fear of not being able to support herself was overcome when she took a leap of faith, left her job, and pursued her dream. Veronica found that in the tough times, she was able to make ends meet by doing other things she loved to supplement her acting and writing. She cooked for others, consulted, and created art. As she pursued her passion, Veronica began to live a life of no regrets.

- Remember, you are loved.
- Remember, you and your contributions are significant. Your community and your world need your gifts.
- Remember, your resources are on loan to you from God.
- Remember, you are here to make the world a better place.
- Remember to share.
- Remember to love.
- Remember, you are a financial genius.
- Remember, you are a beloved child of God.